A Still,
Small
Voice

Other books by Echo Bodine

Echoes of the Soul
Hands That Heal
Relax! It's Only a Ghost

A Still, Small Voice

A Psychic's Guide to Awakening Intuition

Echo L. Bodine

NEW WORLD LIBRARY
NOVATO, CALIFORNIA

New World Library
14 Pamaron Way
Novato, California 94949
www.newworldlibrary.com

Copyright © 2001 by Echo L. Bodine
Edited by Marc Allen and Caroline Pincus
Cover design by Peri Poloni
Text design by Tona Pearce Myers

Library of Congress Cataloging-in-Publication Data
Bodine, Echo L.
A still, small voice : a psychic's guide to awakening intuition /
Echo L. Bodine.
  p.   cm.
ISBN 1-57731-136-1 (alk. paper)
1. Intuition (Psychology) I. Title.
BF315.5 .B63 2001
153.4'4—dc21   00-013267

First Printing, May 2001
ISBN 1-57731-136-1
Printed in Canada on acid-free paper
Distributed to the trade by Publishers Group West

10 9 8 7 6 5 4 3

I would like to dedicate this book to my very gifted chiropractor,
Dr. Marcie New, who has been incredibly supportive of me
and my work during the writing of all my books.
Marcie, you've held my body together during some very tough times
and taught me so much about my physical health
and my soul's well-being.
Thanks so much for being such a dear and loving friend.

*The intuitive mind
is a sacred gift
and the rational mind
is a faithful servant.
We have created a society
that honors the servant
and has forgotten the gift.*

— Albert Einstein

Table of Contents

Acknowledgments

To my mom, Mae Bodine, for teaching me to live this way of life. To Caroline Pincus, my wonderful editor on this project. I was so grateful when I heard you were available for this book, because you're not only a very gifted editor, you're an absolute delight to work with. Thanks for all your insights and suggestions and for providing some of the quotes for the book.

To Marc Allen, Munro Magruder, Georgia Hughes, and Marjorie Conte for all your efforts getting my work out there. Thanks for believing in my abilities and for being such a strong supportive force in my life.

To my fiancé, Mike Hartley, for being so understanding about the things I feel called to do. You are always so patient and understanding and I feel really blessed to have you in my life. Thanks a million, honey.

To my son Kurt, for being in my life and for always doing the research for my books. I love you, baby.

A Still, Small Voice

And he said, Go forth, and stand upon the mount
before the Lord. And, behold, the Lord passed by,
and a great and strong wind rent the mountains,
and brake in pieces the rocks before the Lord;
but the Lord was not in the wind:
and after the wind an earthquake;
but the Lord was not in the earthquake:
and after the earthquake a fire;
but the Lord was not in the fire:
and after the fire a still, small voice.

— Elijah in 1 Kings 19:11, 12

Introduction

As a psychic, I get hundreds of calls every year from people looking for guidance. Some are desperate, others are simply curious, and their questions are as varied as they are. They come to me trying to understand the reasons for health challenges or problems with relationships; they're looking for guidance on career choices or parenting issues; wanting to unblock childhood memories or the root causes of their depression; wanting to discover the psychological, physical, or soul reasons behind weight problems, abuse, sexual dysfunction, addictions, or trauma. Some of them want help accessing information about past lives or communicating with the deceased.

I enjoy what I do and believe my work can be very beneficial to people, but there are times when I wonder if I might not be doing my clients a *dis*service by answering all their questions. I worry that I'm enabling their dependence on outside sources rather than encouraging them to go within and seek their own answers. So many of their questions — when is this new guy going to call, am I going to win the lottery, which car should I purchase, when should I move, should I get an abortion, what school should my child go to? — are questions their own intuition can answer with a simple phrase, or even a simple yes or no. It is the deeper questions that pertain to their soul's path that require the more in-depth information that perhaps only a psychic can give.

There's an old Chinese proverb: "If you give a man a fish he'll eat for a day; teach him how to fish and he'll eat forever." The book you hold in your hand came about because I believe that most of the time it's more important to teach people how to fish than to feed them for a day. I want *you* to learn how to access your own intuition, and to discover how to trust it and use it to live a life of magic and abundance. I'll show you the difference between psychic abilities and intuition, and how psychic readings can keep you dependent on others but living by intuition can set you free.

How I Discovered My Intuition

When I was growing up, I wanted to be just like my mother. She is physically very beautiful and has a loving, giving heart, a great sense of humor, and a certain mystique that makes you wonder if she isn't part gypsy. To top it off, she has always had an uncanny *knowing* about everything that happens in our lives.

As a child I decided that the way to be like her was to do everything just as she did. When she cooked I'd be right beside her in the kitchen. When she baked, I would follow along with my tiny rolling pin, cake pans, and Easy Bake Oven. On the nights when she dressed up to go out with my dad, I would put on some of her clothes, jewelry, and makeup and try to make myself as glamorous as she was. I really did believe that if I did everything just like she did, I'd grow up to be just as beautiful and caring and giving.

I don't recall how old I was when she first introduced me to the idea of listening to my intuition, but I'll never forget that she described it as a "silent voice" inside my stomach that would guide me through life. But whereas my mother is a highly unusual, mystical Moonchild (a Cancer, on the cusp of Leo), I'm a Virgo and very much a product of our culture and our times, which means I'm a thinker — left brained, logical, practical, and down to earth. So the idea of trusting a voice other than the one in my head seemed a little too wacky to me at the time. I put women's intuition in the same category as old wives' tales; intuition wasn't based on facts that could be proven, so I had a hard time believing in its significance. Still, the fact that she attributed her incredible ability to always *know* what was going on to her "intu," as she called it, really got my attention.

Whenever I'd ask for guidance, she would refer me to my intuition. Learning to listen to this voice in my stomach came in gradual stages, and my logical mind fought it all the way.

Fortunately for me, Mom didn't get discouraged by my skeptical attitude. She just kept right on recommending that I go within for my answers. Many times I felt caught in the conflict between what my head thought I should do and the guidance I was receiving from my inner voice, but over time it became perfectly clear: whenever I let the inner voice guide me, life always seemed to work out. The decisions I made would turn out right not only for me, but for others as well. I'd end up in the right place at the right time and so many "coincidences" kept happening that it became a way of life.

It wasn't until I was twenty-five and in recovery from alcoholism that I began to think there might really be something substantial to all this talk about intuition. I was reading the Big Book of Alcoholics Anonymous, the basic text of the twelve-step program, and came across the promises of sobriety. One of them is, "We will intuitively know how to handle situations which used to baffle us." That had a great impact. There it was in the Big Book — trust your intuition. That made me pay attention to it even more.

It took about ten more years, however, before I made the connection between the voice I'd come to rely on and the "still, small voice" mentioned in the Bible. And it took a few more years to realize that this loving, gentle, subtle voice at the center of my being was actually the voice of God within me!

I've now come to see intuition as humankind's best kept secret. The wondrous thing about it is that everyone has it; the trouble is so few of us know how sacred and powerful it is.

Now, in spite of the road blocks my mind tries to put up from time to time — mainly doubt and fear — I am consciously working at living by my inner voice. I conduct my day-to-day affairs by its guidance. I pay my bills by it. I write books by it and send them to the publisher it guides me to. My intuition tells me which gas station to go to for service and nudges me when the mechanic is trying to sell me something I don't need. When I'm looking for a gift for someone, it guides me to the right store and the perfect present. (People are always asking me, "How did you know I wanted this?") If I need to get hold of someone, it tells me when they're home or in the office.

It has guided every business decision I've ever made, told me where and when to look for a house, and when and where to take a trip. It guides me with my health, showing me which doctor to see and which herbs or medications to take. It lets me know which Sundays I should go to church and which Sundays I can sleep in. It tells me how much to tithe and when. Who to date and not to date. Which speakers to listen to, which books to read, which route to drive, who I can trust and who I need to be careful of. When I listen to it, my inner voice is always right there to give me the guidance and direction I need in every area of my life.

Over the next eight chapters, I'll share with you just about everything I know about intuition. In chapter 1, I'll explain what intuition is, where it's located, what it sounds like. In chapter 2, we'll take a look at the other internal voices that can interfere with our ability to hear the divine guidance within us — the voices of our parents, grandparents, peers, therapists, significant others, religion, society, as well as of our emotions such as fear, guilt, shame, hopelessness, despair.

In chapter 3, we'll explore the differences between psychic abilities and intuition and separate myth from fact about them both. In chapter 4, I share some very simple, practical steps to help you listen to and live by the still, small voice within, and in chapter 5 we'll look at some of the resistance you may encounter as you start living this way of life. Many people around us often feel that we've rocked the boat when we start acting from our intuition, and this chapter offers some practical advice for dealing with that.

In chapter 6, I'll discuss the importance of timing and listening to the "Big Ben of the Universe," and in chapter 7, we'll talk about living one day at a time and how it not only eliminates stress but helps us to live rich, full lives. As a little bonus, I've included chapter 8, which shares a few of the many stories I've collected about the magic that happens when people are willing to listen to loving signs from the Universe.

If I have done my job well, by the end of the book you will have made friends with your own "still, small voice" and you will already have experienced the gracious wisdom we all have within us. Your intuition can be your constant companion, and it will always guide you to your highest good.

A Still,
Small
Voice

Chapter 1

Humanity's Best-Kept Secret

Trust your hunches.
They're usually based on facts
filed away just below the conscious level.

— Dr. Joyce Brothers

A few years ago, my boyfriend and I were heading out for a boat trip on the St. Croix River in Wisconsin for three days. The weather forecast was that it would be in the low 90s, so I was packing shorts and sleeveless tops, but my intuition kept nudging me to bring my sweats. My logical self argued my intuitive self out of bringing the sweats and, wouldn't you know it, two days later a cold front came in from Canada and I huddled inside the boat with Mike's sweats on. My head said one thing but, as usual, my inner voice knew better.

Think back to the last time you heard yourself say, I *knew* I should have gone that way, or I *knew* I was going to run into so

and so, or I *knew* who was on the phone. Maybe you were looking at new cars, and even though the car you wanted looked and
sounded great, you just had a feeling, a hunch, something inside
that told you not to buy it. Maybe you *just got a feeling* that the
time was right to call that prospective client and you ended up
making a great sale with hardly any effort. Or you were driving
home and your head wanted you to take the freeway but you just
knew that this time you should take the slower surface streets,
only to end up getting a flat tire right across the street from a gas
station! Remember that feeling of *knowing*? That's your intuition,
the inner wisdom that says take the alternate route, don't buy this
car, cancel the trip, make the call.

If you child isn't feeling well, your inner voice will tell you if

Every time you act on these "illogical" feelings you are working from intuition. People often ask me why they should bother
listening to their inner voice when their life is going fine as it is,
living by their intellect. My answer is simple: Life is not only more
magical when we live by our inner voice but also extremely effi-
cient. From the life-changing to the mundane, your intuition is
always your best guide.

If your child isn't feeling well, your inner voice will tell you if
it's serious or something that will pass. When you can't decide
whether to take the bus to work or drive, your inner voice will
steer you right. If you can't figure out what to wear to that important business meeting, your intuition will help you decide. When
you need to buy a present but haven't got a clue what to get, your
inner voice will always guide you to the perfect gift. If you've read

about a great new herb on the market that can get rid of cellulite but don't know if you should try it, trust your intuition. It's always right.

Why? I have come to believe that it's because intuition is that part of us that is connected to the divine. When our souls were created, the source that created us took a part of its energy and breathed eternal life into us. This part of us is commonly referred to as our Higher Self or the God within.* This voice of God, which the Bible refers to as a "still, small voice" (1 Kings 19:12) is our guide, our compass, our way shower, our intuition.

When our head is guiding us, we *think* we know what's going on, but when we're being guided by intuition, we *know* what's going on. And that knowing comes from the place within us that is connected to our source. Whenever we get that *feeling*, "I *knew* that was going to happen," "I *knew* who was on the phone," "I *knew* I was going to run into so and so today," "I *knew* I was going to get a raise," " I *knew* that publisher would accept my manuscript," we're talking about intuition.

It's not a chatty voice or an intellectual voice and, in fact, it doesn't really come in the form of sound. It's more like a thought that comes from inside your stomach. It's usually quick and to the point. Sometimes, especially when we're still in the process of discovering and hearing the voice, its answers are simply yes, no, or wait. But the more we develop a relationship with this divine

---

* I go into this in depth in my book *Echoes of the Soul.*

part of ourselves, the longer the communication gets. We begin to "hear" full sentences, even paragraphs, of guidance.

The Problem with God

Many people who begin to explore these life-changing things get hung up with the whole concept of God. They don't know what to believe about God, so they just stay away from Him/Her/It altogether. Or they only reach out to God in times of trouble. And they certainly don't relate to the idea of having a divine presence within themselves.

Many of us go to church or synagogue every week, do the rituals we've been taught, say the memorized prayers at the appropriate times, and believe that the hour per week we spend "worshipping God" is all that we need to have a fulfilling intimate relationship with our creator. But look at it this way: If you're trying to have a relationship with someone but only see them once a week for about twenty minutes (we're subtracting time here for weekly announcements, choir time, collection plate time, greeting and good-bye time, and so on), it's absurd.

We all know that in order to have a successful relationship with someone, we need to work at it. To develop intimacy, we need to keep the lines of communication open. We need to talk and listen, give and receive, throughout the whole week. Developing a fulfilling relationship with God is no different.

It's about communicating on a daily basis, not just when there's a crisis.

As my minister, Rev. Ken Williamson, said in one of his Sunday morning sermons, God's number isn't 911. If we truly want to walk a fulfilling spiritual path we have to develop a deeper relationship with God. We can't just turn to God in times of crisis.

But often when we try to develop a relationship with God, all sorts of uncomfortable emotions come roaring to the surface, including fear, anger, and confusion. We're afraid of God's power; we're angry that He/She hasn't been there for us at some critical time; we're confused about what we can expect. And for most of us, religion hasn't done such a good job of clarifying this. Instead of empowering us at an early age to develop our own personal relationship with God, organized religion has taught us that God is removed from us, distant from us — and for many of us the image hasn't been very loving.

Periodically I teach a class on living by our intuition, and at the beginning of every class I have everyone take turns sharing an experience they had during the past week when they listened to their intuition. In one particular class, as we made our way around the circle, I noticed that 90 percent of the class was telling stories about *not* acting on the guidance they had received from their intuition. I pointed that out, and asked them to explain to me why they were choosing *not* to follow their intuition. We ended up having a great discussion that led to our religious views of God, and so many of them expressed a fear of what their intuition might tell them to do if they asked for guidance.

They went on to say that as much as they wanted to live fulfilled, spiritual lives, they worried about what course their lives might take if they really did follow the guidance of their intuition. Many realized that they were looking at their intuition in a religious way, fearing what God might ask them to do. The common fear seemed to be that life would be "no more fun, just a lot more hard work." What became clear to me was that if someone wanted to live by her intuition and if her current relationship with God was based on religion, she would first need to heal her old image of God because it was getting in the way of trusting her inner voice.

We've been taught horrible images of a vengeful, spiteful, jealous, schizophrenic guy up in the sky who decides who gets cancer, whose turn it is to die, who's going bankrupt, who's going to be in a car accident, whose house will be hit by a tornado, whose child will be molested, which town will be flooded, which farmers will lose all their crops. He turns up the heat in the South in the summertime and the cold in the North in the wintertime. He causes hurricanes on the East coast and earthquakes in the West. He doesn't make women thin when they pray to lose weight and he doesn't grow hair on men's heads when they pray to stop going bald. He makes it rain on our wedding day, and causes the tire to go flat on the car. He doesn't prevent the teenager from getting pregnant, doesn't heal our favorite pet when it gets sick, and takes our favorite grandma away from us because He wants her home with Him. Worse yet, He has created an eternal paradise for the best and most faithful of his children, and the rest are cast into an eternal hell.

No wonder we struggle so much with trusting this deity. He sounds like a monster.

The relationship I've developed with God through prayer (talking) and meditation (listening) has shown me that this old-time notion of God couldn't be further from the truth. Even though it may be challenging and difficult, each of us needs to set aside the information we've received through our religious training and *find out for ourselves* the truth about our creator.

If you are one of those people who has issues with God, I'd like you to take some some time to write out everything that comes to your mind when you think of the word *God*. Include memories, feelings, experiences you've had that related to God in some way.

Remember, your goal in doing this is to have an open line of communication between you and your higher self, and in order to get that communication as clear as possible, you have to clear the doorway of old rubble so the door can open wide. I can assure you that once you can get rid of the garbage and find the voice inside and begin developing a real relationship with it, you'll discover how completely loving and supportive it is. It will always bring you ease and lightness — but first the old pain has to be healed.

Right now, if you can, get out a journal or notebook and just write out all the thoughts, feelings, memories, resentments, and so on that come to mind when you think of God.

Now I want you to visualize giving this list to God, and to ask for the healing of all this pain. If you would feel better taking the list to a clergy person and sharing it with him or her, do that instead. Your objective here is to forgive God for all the pain you believe He/She has caused you, and to move forward with your relationship with the divine within you.*

Continue to pray for healing daily until you feel a shift internally. You'll know when you've forgiven God and can open that door. It may not happen overnight but, believe me, it will happen. Whenever we pray for healing, our prayers are answered.

The guidance available to us through our intuition can help in every area of our lives: love, money, health, business, or whatever else concerns you.

Intuition and Your Love Life

A friend of mine decided she wanted to take some active steps toward having a fulfilling intimate relationship in her life. She thought of investing money in a dating service or putting an ad in the personals, but whenever she asked her inner voice for guidance,

---

* If you don't have a clergy person to talk to, I would suggest calling Silent Unity Prayer Tower in Lee's Summit, Missouri (800) 669-7729 and ask for their prayers of healing.

she got nothing. One day while she was running errands she had a strong inner feeling to visit her mother. It was a little out of her way, and she didn't have much time, but her gut feeling was so strong, she decided to follow it. While she was there, an old acquaintance of the family unexpectedly stopped by, and they both felt an immediate attraction to one another. They began dating and were married nine months later.

Your intuition will guide you with all questions concerning your love life — where you'll meet the next significant person in your life, who you should and shouldn't date, who you should and shouldn't marry, when it's time to break off a relationship, and when you should stay with it.

If you're searching for your soulmate and wondering if you should join a dating service, go to a singles group at a local church, or search the bars for Mr. or Ms. Right, just listen to what your inner voice tells you to do rather than doing what everyone else is doing. I think of it as the Universal Matchmaker. Here's a story of how it worked for me:

I was driving home from a meeting one afternoon and my inner voice told me to stop at the grocery store *now* and call a friend. When my inner voice tells me to stop and make a phone call *now*, it usually means the phone and the person are both available, so it struck me as odd when I went into the store and there were two men standing in line to use the phone. At first I wondered if I had misread my intuition, but it was so adamant that I stop *now* that I decided to be patient and see what happened.

The man in front of me turned around and asked me if I was in a hurry to use the phone. I told him I wasn't and that I'd wait until he was done. He smiled at me and said he hoped I had a nice day, and then said by all means go ahead and use the phone. At that he walked away. I was so struck by his gentleness and his smile that I thought about it on and off throughout the day.

The next day, during my morning meditation, my inner voice told me to go to that same store for some seafood, so I made a mental note to stop there on my errands. When I got to the meat and fish counter at the store, there was the man with the smile — it turns out he was a butcher who worked there. We had a friendly little chat, and we ended up seeing each other seriously for about five years.

That's just how it works when intuition is trying to help us meet someone. If you want to meet someone significant, you need to tell God you're ready and then you need to pay attention. Your inner voice will give you a nudge to call so and so, or maybe direct you to go to a certain place, or join a specific dating service, or put an ad in the paper. It nudges us through our gut feelings to take the steps we need to in order to meet that certain someone.

For people in relationships, intuition gives great suggestions about how to keep them going strong and working well. Communication is a huge part of a relationship, and your intuition will help you know when and what to say and when to listen. It's an amazing helper, and our best teacher.

For those that are thinking of getting out of a relationship, I strongly suggest that you consult your intuition first. Many times we end up in certain relationships to deal with unfinished business, from this life and from past lives. If you get out before the karma is worked out, you'll just end up back in the relationship again, or repeating the same mistakes over and over in other relationships. That's why some couples break up so many times before finally ending it. Your intuition will let you know when the timing is right to get in or get out of a relationship.

Intuition and Business

Stories of intuition in business are legendary. Every successful business is based on an intuitive impulse that was acted upon. I've had my own business since 1979, and I've consulted my inner voice for just about every decision I've had to make — from hiring a secretary to planning future classes. I've never had to put an ad in the paper for a secretary. Whenever I need assistance, I ask God (usually out loud, but silence works fine too) to bring me the perfect person for my business needs, and usually within a week the right person walks into my life and my inner voice nudges me to pay attention. I always ask my intuition what to pay them and each time an amount comes through clearly. No one has ever argued with me about salary. When my first secretary needed to quit for personal reasons, within days my inner voice guided me to the next secretary, who had been getting an inner feeling that she was going to be working for me before we even chatted. When it was time for her to move on, my inner voice nudged me to call a friend of mine, and it turned out his sister was looking for a job.

The key for all of us is to still our minds and not panic. Our heads usually go right to all the things we *should* do — put an ad in the paper, call an agency, etc. — but none of that may be necessary if we listen to the still, small voice within.

If you have your own business, your intuition will help you with every decision you have to make, from ordering inventory to scheduling projects and important meetings, deciding when and who to hire and fire, finding the right accountant, the perfect attorneys, which supplier to go with, which internet server to go with, when to have the company picnic, and which clients you want to work with and which ones to pass on. When you can get in the habit of focusing on the internal voice within your stomach area, *not* your head, you'll feel it correctly nudging you with all the decisions you need to make.

My intuition always serves me well in planning new classes, setting up appointments, planning business trips, and teaching workshops. Anything that requires a decision about timing is especially important to run by my "intuitive consultant," because the source within knows so much more than my head — in fact, it seems to know everyone who's interested in taking my classes and their schedules, the weather conditions coming up, the other activities that might be taking place at the facility I'm going to rent, what my energy is going to be like, and the other events coming up in my life that I don't know about yet.

In spite of what my head might say about the best time to schedule these things, I always go by my inner voice. I've learned the hard way that if I schedule something according to my head and haven't checked in intuitively, I never have the good results I was hoping for. Our inner voice always knows what's best for us and our circumstances, and so it's the perfect business partner. Intuition/God comes up with the great ideas; all we have to do is carry them out.

It's important to realize that we're all connected. When you speak to your inner voice about a need you have, the other people who are involved will also get a nudge from their inner voice, and it will all come together like a big jigsaw puzzle. Living by intuition is a magical way to live.

Intuition is also a great career counselor. Several years ago, I was intuitively led to visit a friend of mine in Malibu. Several "coincidences" happened over a short two-day stay, and I ended up with a job at the Malibu Health Club, doing healings and readings. The club told me I was welcome to work there as often as I wanted to, and whenever I wanted to. Instead of pulling up stakes, moving to Malibu, and setting up a regular schedule, which many of my friends said I should do, I left it up to my inner voice to tell me when I should go to California.

I ended up flying out from time to time for just a few days work, and it always went extremely well. Many people asked why I didn't move out there because I had more business there than I knew what to do with, but I knew I had to trust my inner voice and go when I was guided. Periodically I would "check in" intuitively to see if it was time to go back to Malibu, and only when I got a clear yes would I get out the calendar. I'd look at all the coming weeks and ask my intuition self if I should go this week, or this week, or that, and I could always count on my inner voice to give me that strong yes feeling when the time was right.

One visit will always rank high in my tales of intuition. It was the end of the fall in 1995, and my inner voice was adamant that I should go to Malibu during one particular week in December. It even told me clearly that the Friday of that week was the reason I was going. It said that a dark-haired man with intense eyes would be coming for a session on Friday afternoon and that after my session with him I could come home because the reason for the trip would be over.

By the time I arrived at the club on Tuesday of that week, there were women clients booked Tuesday, Wednesday, and Thursday, but Friday was still completely open. As usual my head got in there and started to question whether I had heard things right about the timing — perhaps I had only wanted to trade the cold Minnesota winter for a few sunny days by the ocean. Whenever I checked in intuitively to hear if I had read it accurately, my inner voice would say, "*Friday, 4:00, then you can go home.*"

By the time I left the club on Thursday evening there was still no one on the books for Friday, but when I arrived back where I was staying, my inner voice said to call the club and double check Friday's schedule. I called right away and the woman at the desk said a man had just come in and booked an appointment for Friday at 4:00. I asked if he had dark hair and intense eyes. She laughed and said he sure did! Then told me his name, and I was blown away — not only did he match my intuition's description, he was a movie star I had always wanted to meet! I was so excited I could hardly sleep that night. My fears got in the way as well: What if I couldn't read him, what if no healing energy came out of my hands, and how on earth could I lose thirty pounds and a face full of wrinkles by 4:00 P.M.?

I checked in with my intuition to be sure I could work on this man without losing it, and the guidance came through that I needed to take this very seriously. I had to remember to stop being star-struck and give him what *he* needed. Before the session, I cleared myself (you'll see how to do that in chapter 4), and I was able to get focused and bring through the important information he needed to hear. When the session was over, he hugged me and gave me a kiss on the cheek (my knees were shaking!), and said it was hard for him to find a psychic who didn't just kiss his sweet behind and tell him what he wanted to hear. He thanked me over and over for being so direct with him.

Before he left, we exchanged phone numbers and he asked me to autograph one of my books for him! Never in my wildest imagination would I have thought that this movie star would end up asking for *my* autograph! When he left, my inner voice said, "*You can go home now.*" I felt elated and peaceful at the same time. Once again, I had honored the voice within and it turned out well for everyone concerned.

Seven months passed before my intuition sent me out to Malibu again, and at the end of that week my inner voice told me I was done coming to Malibu. It said I needed to concentrate on all the work I had back home in Minnesota. At the same time, a lot of people in my life were advising me to spend *more* time in Malibu or even to move out there, but I listened to the voice that knew me and my path the best. Once I closed the door on Malibu, wonderful new work opportunities opened up back home, which was a clear indication that I was on the right track.

By listening to my internal voice regarding all my business decisions, I've always ended up in the right place at the right time, meeting the right people and doing the right thing.

Intuition and Money

When I suggest to people that they trust their inner voice to guide them in all their money matters, they usually think I've gone off the deep end. Nothing seems to push most people's fear buttons more than money. For a lot of people, money represents security, and for others it represents power. Underneath our need for both security and power is, of course, fear. Many people think that money is more powerful than God and that if they have enough money, they don't need God.

Another thing about the green stuff that makes it difficult for many of us is the belief that money and spirituality are arch enemies. So many people believe that to walk a true spiritual path, they must be paupers, thereby proving that their allegiance is to God. This belief couldn't be further from the truth, but it can take lifetimes for us to learn that.

Our religion has taught many of us that money is the root of all evil — and it certainly can be. It can be a source of jealousy and envy, and it can cause people to cheat each other, steal, run scams, hate, con, and lie. It causes divorces, murders, robbery, and prison time.

But when we look at what Christianity really teaches, we see that Jesus said that money is simply a medium of exchange and that our daily needs will all be met if we simply trust. The truth is, your inner voice will make much wiser decisions regarding your money than you ever will because it knows all the financial needs, wants, and responsibilities you have now and will have in the future. And when the inner voice is guiding you financially, any issues you may have about low self-worth don't get in the way, because your intuition wants nothing but the best for you! It's our negative beliefs about ourselves that keep us in financial straits, not God.

Our intuition is the most powerful weapon we have against all the fears we may have, including the fears at the root of our need for security, power, and money. Sometimes listening to our intuition means going against everything we've been taught about being responsible or sensible. But, your intuition will never let you down.

There have been many times I've gone to pay a bill before its due date and my inner voice has told me to wait. Or I've been at a store thinking about making a purchase and my inner voice says *no,* even though I've got the money and there is no apparent reason why I can't or shouldn't buy it. Or my head says it's time to take the car in for an oil change and the voice says *not today.*

Every time I've rebelled against the voice I've paid a price. When we're about to make a purchase and our intuition tells us *no* or *wait,* it usually means one of the following: The money we've earmarked for one thing will be needed for something else, or the item's about to go on sale, or there might be a much better option coming that we don't know about yet, or we don't need what we think we want and won't end up using it at all.

When you need to make a decision regarding anything having

to do with money, run it by your intuition. *Ask* the questions and then focus on the area around your gut. There will be an inner nudge when you ask. Here are some examples:

- Should I invest in such and such?

- Can I make this purchase?

- Should I file bankruptcy?

- Can I afford to go on vacation, and when should I go?

- How much and who should I tithe money to?

- Is that nasty letter from the IRS something I need to take seriously?

- How much should I put in savings?

Focus on your gut feeling. Is it giving you a *yes, no,* or *wait?* If you're emotionally involved in the decision, walk away from it for a while. When you feel you've calmed down, focus your attention on the area of your gut once again, and ask your question. Once you get the hang of this, feeling that inner knowingness will get easier and easier.

If you're having financial problems and can't afford to pay all your bills, ask your intuition which ones need paying now and which ones can wait. Any and all financial decisions can be made through your intuition. It's like having your own personal banker in your front pocket at all times, except this one loves you unconditionally, knows what's coming up for you, *and* doesn't charge a monthly fee for all that advice.

As you work on trusting your intuition with your finances, a lot of old fears, old religious beliefs, and low self-worth will probably surface. Don't let those obsolete fears and beliefs gum up the progress you're making with your intuition. Write them out in a journal, talk them over with a trusted friend, and please see them for what they are: old saboteurs that have been in your way for years.

Intuition and Health

Wouldn't it be nice if your car had a built-in voice that was directly connected to the manufacturer and advised you about its condition and maintenance at all times — and if a problem did occur, it would give you immediate answers as to what to do? Unfortunately our cars aren't there yet, but guess what? Our bodies are! They have an inner voice that comes directly from the manufacturer and knows the condition of our bodies at all times and what they need for upkeep and smooth running.

Your intuition knows your body from head to toe and will advise you any time you seek its advice. It'll advise you on what to eat, what supplements you need, and how much rest to get. It will guide you to the right doctors and the correct treatment you need, should a problem arise. Remember, all you need to do is ask and then listen.

As you can see, there's nothing in your life that intuition *can't* help. And it's so simple: you have access to divine wisdom twenty-four hours a day, seven days a week. In chapter 4 I'll give you some tips and tools for *how* to live intuitively, but as we close this chapter, I hope I've convinced you that your intuition really is your best ally and your key to living a more enchanted life. Whether or not things are working well for you right now, your intuition can always give you an effortless boost.

Chapter 2

The Other Voices

Look within, and you'll find
every answer you need
Look within, and you'll find
an ever-ripened seed
Watch it grow! Watch it grow!
we're but seeds in the earth
Watch it bloom, watch it flower
every moment is rebirth

— *Marc Allen*

Several years ago, a very dear friend called and asked if I would channel healings to her fourteen-year-old stepson who had fallen eighteen feet, landed on his head, and was in a coma at one of our local hospitals. Just as I arrived at his room, I overheard the nurse telling his family that the chances of him ever coming out of the coma were very slim, and she suggested putting him in a nursing home to save on expenses. Everyone was filled with fear, including me, and I knew I had to get away from that room and talk to God.

I walked down the hall and asked my inner guidance what I should do. Should I channel healings to this boy or accept what the nurse had just said and leave it alone? I clearly heard my inner voice ask, *"Are you going to listen to the fears of the world or are you going to get to work?"* The words came with certainty and calmness, and I knew it was my intuition — I knew it was for the highest good of all, I knew it was God.

For the next six weeks, whenever I channeled healing to this boy, I concentrated only on my inner voice for guidance. Whenever there was any discouraging news from the medical staff, or fear going on with the family, I would leave the room and check in with God. Sometimes it was hard to focus on the positive calm feeling within when all outside indications seemed so bleak. It took a lot of discipline to detach from the fear and anger in the voices all around me and to listen to the one true voice within, but practicing that kind of detachment has turned out to be one of the most valuable learning experiences I've ever had as a healer. Six weeks after the nurse told the family to put this young coma victim in a nursing home, he walked out of the hospital on his own and went back to living a normal life.

The Other Voices

The trouble is that most of us have so many different voices inside that it's hard to know which one is God's. Over the course of our lives, we internalize the voices of so many others — parents, siblings, friends, our inner child — and we deem them conscience. There are all the voices from society, the church, our teachers, the government, our bosses, the neighbors, our significant other, that tell us what to do in any given situation. And then there are all the internalized voices of the various emotions we experience, such as fear, anger, or sadness. All these voices can mask what the inner voice is trying to say.

Maybe you're so angry at your boss for not giving you a raise that you think your inner voice is telling you to quit and leave him high and dry — but that's anger speaking, not intuition. Guilt or shame (often interpreted as conscience) are two of the most insidious voices that can masquerade as intuition. We all know too well how persistent they can be. And then there's the most dominant voice of all, in most of us: the intellect, the voice of reason, logic, common sense, and practicality. All of these voices chatter away inside us throughout the day, and they can cause an awful lot of static and confusion.

In this chapter, we're going to look at how to recognize the difference between the inner voice that connects you to the Universe and these other voices that interfere with that connection.

How to Distinguish Intuition

Here's a simple test for distinguishing if an internal message is coming from your intuition or from one of the other voices: Ask yourself if there's an emotion attached to it. When the inner voice speaks, no matter what it has to tell us, it's always calm and without emotion. Even when a message appears to be negative, if you can calm yourself down and really listen, you'll sense the calmness in the voice and *know* that your intuition is speaking.

I was on my way to the doctor one day and as I was driving I was thinking of the questions I wanted to ask him. With absolute calm, my inner voice said "*no,*" which of course took me by surprise. I asked it what "no" meant, and I then heard the word "*accident.*" Although there was a calm feeling with it, I went into a panic. "What do you mean accident? What kind of *accident?* Can I avoid it?" No answer came, so I stayed very alert to everything around me — and while sitting at a stop sign I was rear ended by a drunk driver.

If I had thought about an accident and then felt a rush of fear in my stomach, I would have known it was one of my fears popping up and not my intuition. You might be thinking that an accident is a terrible thing and my intuition should have helped me avoid it, but what's interesting here is that the accident eventually ended up playing a major role in my own healing process, so I know it was meant to be.

Let's look at some other situations in which the chorus of

other voices might kick in: Say you want to purchase a new car. You go to the dealership and the salesman pushes hard for you to buy the souped-up model with all the extras. His pitch makes sense and the vehicle he's showing you seems pretty practical given that it gets great mileage and the trunk is big enough to haul the equipment you use for work. You ask your inner voice for guidance and up pops the phrase, "Way too impractical for someone your age." But those words have a judgmental quality to them, and so you're able to recognize that it's your mother's voice speaking, and not your intuition. Then you hear grandma saying she'd never ride in that thing 'cause it's too big. Dad's voice wants to know how you're going to pay for it, and your best friend's voice interjects that he thinks it's totally cool and wants to know if he can borrow it. Then comes a voice from somewhere or other telling you that you don't deserve it because you haven't worked hard enough for it. This loud chorus makes it almost impossible to hear your inner voice, which will either be saying a simple but firm *yes, buy it,* or *no.*

Sometimes when there are too many voices and too much pressure, you just have to take a walk and ask God to clear you of all the chattering voices and help you see what's best in this situation. Just focus on your gut and ask, "Should I buy this vehicle? Yes or no?" You'll get a feeling, an inner knowing, when you ask and pay attention to the answer, and it will always feel like the right thing to do. God knows what your future finances and responsibilities are going to be, knows if you're going to get a raise or lose your job. He/She also knows if there's a better price or better vehicle somewhere else. Or perhaps He/She has a different plan entirely (which will always be for your highest good). And by the way, God would never tell you you don't deserve something. It's not in God's vocabulary. Jesus said, "Ask and you shall receive." He didn't say, "Ask and you shall receive — if you deserve it."

Another example: You're self-employed and it's time to mail in your estimated taxes. You get a very calm, strong feeling inside that you shouldn't send in the money at this time — but then the voices take over: Your spouse's voice tells you you're being irresponsible; the government's voice says you'll pay heavy fines or maybe even go to jail if you don't send it in; the practical side of you reminds you that you can't afford the interest and penalties you have to pay if you don't send the money in on time; and society's voice says, "Hey, we have to pay our taxes, why shouldn't you? There are two certainties in life, right? Death and taxes." Even though you still *feel* strongly that you shouldn't mail in the money, you go ahead and send it in, and two days later you break your foot in a skiing accident or a family member becomes seriously ill and you need to take time off from work to take care of her, or any of a million other scenarios could occur and now you're in quite a jam because you didn't listen to the inner guidance and you have no money set aside to support yourself or your family.

Here's another example: Your child tells you he's sick and wants to stay home from school. You ask your inner voice for guidance on what to do — send Junior to school or let him stay home — and all you can hear are the voices of the world: Your mother harps at you for making your career more important than your child; your husband says you baby him enough as it is, make him go to school; the school nurse says what kind of a mother are you for sending a sick child to school; and your guilt kicks in for even *thinking* of going to work. Instead of recognizing that these are other people's opinions, or seeing your guilt for what it is, instead of calming yourself down and going deeper within yourself to the place of truth, where your intuition is saying, "Junior isn't that sick and can go to school, just spend some good quality time with him in the evening, now go to work and fulfill the other obligations you have," you decide it's easier to just take the day off and not fight with all the voices in your head. But when we don't listen or we go against the guidance we do hear, there's a nagging feeling in the pit of our stomach that we're not on the right track, and that never feels good. A lot of us try covering up that dissatisfied feeling with alcohol, drugs, food, or any of the other addictions we can get into. When we honor the wisdom of the internal voice, the need for these outside distractions usually stops.

When Going with Your Intuition Feels Selfish

Listening to your intuition can be especially hard for those of you who are primarily caretakers. You want to please everyone and never want to feel responsible for someone having a bad day.

If you are someone who is always taking care of others rather than focusing on yourself, walking the path of intuition is going to require making some major shifts in the way you do things. You're going to have to realize that you're not the one responsible for making life turn out well for all those around you. God loves all the people you love and watches out for them, too. It's not up to you to make sure everyone has a good day.

Taking off your caregiver's hat is kind of like giving up the role of cruise ship director. I know how tough it can be — it may seem downright impossible! It may seem as if everything's going to fall apart. But when we stop deciding what's best for everyone else and focus on ourselves and our inner voice, life becomes so much more manageable, not only for us, but for everyone concerned. You're setting free the people you've been taking care of by encouraging them to go within to their own inner voice. You're no longer feeding people for a day but, by supporting them to discover their own inner guidance, you're teaching them to take care of themselves for a lifetime.

Here's a typical situation a co-dependent person might find herself in: She wakes up on a Sunday morning with low energy and a headache. She gets a strong inner nudging to cancel all her plans for the day and just get some overdue sleep. She lies in bed for a couple of minutes thinking about how wonderful it would be to have the day to herself, but then begins to hear those voices of the world: She hears the voices of the Women's Auxiliary judging her for not being in church; she hears the minister's *tone of voice* the next time he sees her, insinuating her sinfulness at not being in church. She remembers that she promised her neighbor she'd give her a ride, and she stayed up late making brownies for social hour, so no matter how much she wants to stay home and rest, even though her intuition may be telling her to, the *important* voices are more prominent. There's no way she could come home from church and take a well-deserved break because she promised her nephew she'd take him for a driving lesson and told her niece she would sew up the hem on her dress. And she needs to get to the grocery store because she's invited a lonely neighbor to come for dinner.

All she can think about is how disappointed everyone will be if she "selfishly" takes the day off, so rather than upsetting every-one else's day and heeding the wisdom from within, she crawls out of bed, takes a couple of pain pills and an extra vitamin, and goes about her day, pleasing everyone but herself. By not listening to her own inner voice, the vicious co-dependent cycle continues and no one gets set free by going within for divine guidance. Listening to your intuition isn't selfish, it's wise. The people around you may be disappointed when you change your plans, but in the long run, they will understand that you are following your guidance, and you will serve as an example to them, perhaps even an inspiration, showing them how to live by listening to their intuition.

The Most Dominant Voice of Them All

The voice you need to be especially aware of is the voice of your own ever-logical mind. Our minds are trained to think, to reason things out, and to solve problems based on the information that they've gathered. When the mind calculates all possible scenarios and comes up with a decision to turn left and your intuition comes along and says, *"No, go straight,"* the mind isn't prepared to just sit back and submit to this other opinion, which after all wasn't based on any reasonable and logical thought. It's going to resist that quiet little intuitive voice. Our minds have a great deal of pride about being right, and they usually balk — at least in the beginning — when we ask them to stand aside and let intuition come through.

In the beginning, as you're gradually learning to shift gears from listening to your head to listening to the quieter and more certain voice within your gut, your mind may need a little coddling. Talk to it. Be patient and reassure it that it's not being replaced, you're just learning a new way of doing things. Tell it that your goal here is to have the two parts of you work in an exciting partnership with each other, with our intuition receiving inspiration, guidance, and divine wisdom from the Universal mind and our minds then creating and manifesting based on that guidance.

As the years have passed and the quiet inner voice has never misled me, my mind has gotten better at accepting direction from my intuition, but it still occasionally gets irritated and belligerent when the guidance appears to be totally illogical. But remember this: The mind sees things from a limited three-dimensional viewpoint; intuition is based on higher, more comprehensive reasoning. As hard as it is to accept sometimes, it helps to remind your mind that your inner guidance knows what's going on *at all times.* Talk to your mind — tell it that if it would just cooperate with your divine intelligence, the two would make a truly great team.

Yeah, But . . .

Emmet Fox remarked in his daily meditation book that one of the masks Satan wears is the phrase *"yeah, but."* I don't choose to believe his theories about Satan, but I sure know about that phrase he's referring to. *"Yeah, but"* is a competing voice we have to pay particular attention to because these two words will try to sabotage all the positive changes we try to make in our lives.

Try to notice how many times you use those two little words, especially while reading a book like this one. I think you'll be amazed. *"Yeah, but* what would my husband say?" *"Yeah, but* I always do it that way." *"Yeah, but* I don't know how to do that," *"Yeah, but* people won't understand," *"Yeah, but* it's so difficult to change old habits," and on and on it goes. Change is scary, but whenever we hear ourselves saying "yeah, but" we know for certain it is just our fear talking, and we shouldn't let fear stop us from living the life we want to live.

Remember that all the voices within us are just that — voices. They have no power unless we give them power. The one voice we want to empower is our intuitive voice. Don't let the other voices control you or your destiny.

Start today to begin to quiet the other voices so you can hear the still, calm voice of your intuition. Your soul came here for some very specific reasons and your inner voice knows what your soul plan is. Let your higher power work with you and through you to help fulfill what you came here to do. It all works together so well when we take the time to listen to our intuition, and have the courage to follow its guidance.

Chapter 3

Psychic Abilities

*Intuition is a spiritual faculty and does not explain,
but simply points the way.*

— Florence Scovel Shinn

Over the years, many people have commented that I have an obvious advantage when it comes to hearing my intuition because of my psychic abilities. But I always reply — and I feel it's important to understand — that intuition and psychic ability are not the same thing at all. Hearing your intuition has nothing to do with being psychic. They're completely separate. I agree that I've had an advantage to this whole business of living by intuition, but it's not because I have psychic abilities. It's because I was raised by a mother who taught me to live this way. Listening to my inner voice started as far back as I can remember, and there wasn't any formal training. My mother simply said, repeatedly, "Listen to the voice inside," and there were no other instructions. It was simple and to the point. My psychic abilities didn't start until I was seventeen years old. It took two years of psychic development classes and a good twelve years of practicing on friends and family members before I became a professional psychic.

One of the most gifted mediums of our times, James Van Praagh, has the ability to communicate with the deceased and is able to bring incredibly intimate details through from the other side. I've seen James interviewed by many people — Oprah Winfrey, Larry King, Barbara Walters, to name a few — and everyone asks him how he does his work. His standard humble answer is, "It's intuition, and we all have it, and anyone can do what I do." With all due respect to this very gifted man, that's like Mozart or Bach saying, "It's just something I wrote, and anyone could do it." What we see him doing on TV or in his workshops is not just a matter of intuition. He obviously uses intuition to sort through all the profound psychic information he receives or he wouldn't be as accurate as he is, but it's not *just* intuition at work here. He has three powerful psychic gifts as well.

The Three Types of Psychic Ability

There are a great many misconceptions about psychics, psychic abilities, and psychic readings, so I'd like to clarify things as much as possible. Psychic ability is just one of the many talents, gifts, and abilities we were all born with. As with all of our gifts and abilities — creativity, musical ability, healing powers, writing talent, speaking, acting, and so on — it's up to us to decide if we want to develop it or not.

There are actually three distinctly different psychic gifts — clairvoyance, clairaudience, and clairsentience — and how much you've used these abilities in past lives will determine what your strong areas will be in this life. For example, if you developed clairvoyance in a former life, it's going to come a lot easier this time, whereas if this is the first of your lifetimes for clairaudience, it's going to take some time and effort to develop it. Some of the more gifted psychics have all three abilities highly developed, and the majority of them have at least two that have come easily and naturally.

Clairvoyance

Clairvoyance (*clear seeing*) is the gift of seeing visions, images, or pictures. For a clairvoyant, "seeing" psychic information is something like watching a movie. This information comes in through the "third eye," which is located in the middle of the forehead, though invisible to our human eyes. We all have a third eye. As strange as it sounds, this eye can see in every direction. The information received can look something like a cartoon strip. If there's a lot of information, the psychic may get a number of pictures in a sequence, one at a time; other times information comes in as one big picture. Sometimes it comes in slowly, sometimes quickly, depending upon the psychic's ability to see and interpret what she's seeing.

Here's an example of how it works: A client tells a psychic that she's having problems with her marriage but is too close to it to see what the problems really are or to know what she needs to do about them. Up on the psychic's "screen" (another term for the third eye) comes an image of a racetrack. The next frame shows a turtle and a hare at the starting line. In the next picture, the hare takes off going full speed and runs circles around the turtle, who is moving at a very slow but steady pace. The picture seems to emphasize that the turtle is very methodical about its movements and careful to observe and take in everything around her while the hare continues to run in circles, not paying attention to his surroundings. The next picture emphasizes how much the hare wants to win at any cost. He loves to compete with everything. The next picture shows that the turtle is oblivious to the whole concept of winning, she just wants to be aware of what's going on, and to get where she's going.

The clairvoyant receives the information in the form of pictures, and the most important part of the job is to interpret the images as accurately as possible. If a clairvoyant hasn't developed an understanding of the pictures he or she receives, she might give false information. There have been many times in my psychic development (and even now!) when I have misinterpreted the information I receive. It's very important to pay attention to all the details that the pictures are giving us and to interpret them as accurately as possible.

Let's go back to the turtle and the hare. The psychic tells her client what she is seeing, and says that it *feels* like she's the turtle, not being in a hurry to get through life, not feeling competitive, always wanting to stop along the way and enjoy life, while her husband is the hare, going through life like a race, never stopping along the way to enjoy himself but always in a hurry to win. She points out how different they are in their essential nature, and suggests that this is where the problem originates. As you can see, this clairvoyant first received the pictures and then interpreted them according to what she felt the pictures meant, checking out her interpretation with her intuition to more fully understand it before she offered it to her client.

Sometimes the pictures are far more difficult to interpret than at other times. When I get pictures I'm not sure about, I usually describe them in detail to my client and we discuss what they might mean. There's always the possibility that the pictures are not symbolic messages but *actual* scenes from situations that have already occurred, or are currently occurring, or are going to occur in the future. There are two ways to tell: One is to look at every possible interpretation and the other is to check the pictures out intuitively, which we'll talk more about later.

A bit of advice for those of you who get psychic readings: If you've received information that doesn't seem accurate, tell the psychic so. They may not have checked in with their intuition to see if their interpretation was accurate, and they could have simply misinterpreted what they saw. Hopefully they can go back and look at the pictures and see if there's a different explanation.

Clairaudience

The second form of psychic ability is clairaudience (*clear hearing*), the gift of *hearing* spirit. This ability is also located in the head area. I think of it as having psychic ears. There are two ways to hear spirit. One comes through as a clear audible voice, which many people claim to have heard at least once in their life. A voice calls out their name, for instance, but when they look in the direction of the voice they see nothing. The other form of clairaudience, which is the most common, is the ability to "hear" thoughts that come into our head from spirit guides, angels, or our deceased loved ones. If you've ever observed James Van Praagh, John Edward, Sylvia Browne, or any of the other well-known mediums or psychics of our time giving a reading, they're usually having an ongoing conversation with their guides throughout the session. They all have clairaudience. Mental telepathy, which is the ability to pick up thoughts from someone here on earth, is also a form of clairaudience. (My brother Michael calls telepathy pmail. Get it? Psychic mail.)

What makes clairaudience so challenging to the beginner is that all our thoughts and all the different voices seem to sound similar. The more developed the clairaudient's skill becomes, the easier it is to discern among all the thoughts and the different voices coming in. During a psychic reading, a clairaudient can be receiving information from many voices at once: her own spirit guides, the guides of the client, deceased relatives of the client, and perhaps an angel or two. It takes quite a bit of concentration to listen to all the voices and discern which voices are relevant and which are talking gibberish. And although most experienced clairaudients can keep up with the pace, sometimes the thoughts of the spirits come in so quickly that the clairaudient can miss part of the message.

A bit of advice for any of you who might go to see a clairaudient for a reading: You might want to hold your questions and comments until *after* they're done receiving information. It can be pretty tough to discern everything coming in from the different voices while a client is talking as well.

Clairsentience

The third psychic ability is called clairsentience (*clear sensing*). Over the last thirty years the definition of clairsentience has changed. In the past, if a person talked about being clairsentient, it meant they had a "psychic nose," and they got their information through smells, such as smelling a fire that was happening at a great distance or smelling a certain flower associated with a departed loved one. To get our attention, deceased loved ones can sometimes project a smell that was strongly associated with them when they were living — their favorite cologne, for example, or fresh baked cookies. My grandpa's favorite food was vanilla ice cream and, after he passed away, he would project the smell of vanilla ice cream whenever he came to visit me. Later on, when I had developed my psychic abilities, he would simply call my name or appear to me and it was no longer necessary to project the smell.

Today, the definition of clairsentience has changed to mean a broader gift of sensing. It's the ability to sense psychic information. Clairsentients are often referred to as "psychic sponges," because they physically and psychically soak up the environment they're in. They can feel people's health challenges in their own bodies, for instance. As you can imagine, this ability can be a pretty heavy burden. Clairsentients continually need to do clearing exercises to keep themselves clear of other people's *stuff* (which is covered in more detail in chapter 4).

Common Misconceptions about Psychics

I was at a baby shower recently and noticed that the woman sitting next to me was very quiet throughout the afternoon. I didn't know her personally and didn't think much about it until we were just about finished with our meal and she blurted out, "I'm so nervous sitting next to you." I asked her if she thought I could read her mind, and she hesitated and said yes.

As I looked around the table, there were several other women I'd never met before, and I realized that many of them were wondering if I was reading their minds or discovering their deepest secrets. I was so out of my "psychic mode" that day that it hadn't even occurred to me that these women were even thinking of me as being a psychic. I quickly reassured them all that I couldn't and didn't wish to read any of their minds and that their secrets were safe.

There are so many misconceptions about who psychics are and how we use our abilities that I'd like to do my best to lay a few of those misconceptions to rest right here.

Every one of us is unique and different, and psychics are no exception. We all work differently from each other. Some are on a spiritual path, others aren't. Some work with a crystal ball, or read tea leaves or tarot cards, others communicate with angels or spirit guides; some go into a trance and channel their messages, some work with a Ouija Board or do automatic writing. There are mediums who communicate with the dead and others who use their abilities to get rid of ghosts. Some focus strictly on past lives, and others only work with the future. There are aura readers, fortune tellers, and palm readers. Every psychic I know has his or her own unique way of using his or her abilities.

MISCONCEPTION 1: *Psychics can see into the minds of everyone we come into contact with.* It just isn't so. Yes, some psychics are less ethical than others but most professionals turn off their abilities when they're in public. In fact, every hard-working psychic I know will tell you that at the end of a long day of reading people, the last thing he or she wants to do is read people's minds. That's like thinking that bus drivers want to drive people around on their days off!

When I was younger and still developing my abilities, random information would come into my mind about people and it was all very unclear who it was for or about, but as the years passed and I became more psychically developed, I was able to turn my abilities on when I needed them and shut them off when I wasn't using them. Most professional psychics work that way in order to prevent burnout.

It is usually very easy to tell if a person is in the early stages of their psi development. If they've been around awhile, they're respectful of people's boundaries and don't read them unless asked. But those in the beginning stages often get excited and want to show people what they can do, and it can cause problems when they don't wait for people to ask. They "tune into" people to impress or scare them, and that's certainly not what these abilities are for.

If you're ever in a situation like the women at the baby shower, and are uncomfortable in any way because you don't know if a psychic is respecting your boundaries, just ask God to put protection around you, so that no one can read you unless you ask. This is usually not necessary, however, with professional psychics who have been around awhile.

MISCONCEPTION 2: *We all read palms.* I can't tell you how many palms I've had extended to me over the years from people who think all psychics read palms. I don't read them, and neither do most of the psychics I know. Reading palms is a skill palmists learn from a book. You don't need psychic abilities to do it.

MISCONCEPTION 3: *Psychic abilities are evil (or psychics work for Satan).* Maybe back in Biblical times, when there was apparently little or no understanding of psychic abilities, the religious leaders felt that the ability to see into the future could only come from the guy in the red suit with the horns and pitchfork, but it's now two thousand years later and we've learned a lot about the Gifts of Prophesy referred to in 1 Corinthians 12. Jesus and the other prophets in the Old and New Testaments received their visions and messages through clairvoyance and clairaudience. And Jesus told us that we have these abilities as well. "These gifts I give unto you and greater works shall you do." These gifts aren't evil. They are just one of the many gifts and abilities God gave us when we were created.

MISCONCEPTION 4: *Psychics know their own future.* Whenever anything unexpected happens in my life, people always ask me why I didn't know it was going to happen or why my spirit guides didn't warn me about it. In order to see future events, a psychic has to be able to be emotionally detached from their life and to *not* care what's coming. That can be very hard to do in one's own life.

I know that as I've grown spiritually and have come to accept that there's a reason for everything that happens, and as I grow away from a victim mentality and realize that things don't just happen *to* us, sometimes I'm able to see future pictures for myself. And, as I continue on this path, I can hear more in-depth guidance from my intuition as well. But the *key* — and please pay attention to this because this is the key to hearing your intuition as well — is the ability to detach. Psychics can only *see* into personal situations when they are not attached emotionally to the information they might receive.

Psychic Readings

Some of you are probably wondering why anyone would go to a psychic and have no idea what a psychic reading really is. People come to psychics for help with every conceivable kind of life issue. To give you an idea of the kinds of questions people ask psychics, here's a list of questions I've been asked by clients just in the last month.

The codes following each question — [I] for intuition and [PR] for psychic reading — are there to indicate the kinds of questions that can best be answered by our own intuition and the kinds of questions that should be brought to a psychic for a reading. A good psychic can bring through invaluable information to help people on their path but, as I've already stated, I think psychics can keep people stuck and dependent. I really want to encourage you to turn to your own internal guidance whenever possible.

- Will my son be a good student? Should he take the medications the doctors want him to take? What will his grades be? Should we keep him back a year? [I]

- I've had a lot of dental work over the last four years and I'm still in a lot of pain. Can you see what's causing the pain or what I need to do to get rid of it? Will it ever go away? [PR/I] Am I going to the right dentist and, if not, who should I be going to? [I]

- Will I marry the man I'm engaged to? [I]

- Will my father find a part-time job soon? What will he be doing? [PR/I]

- I'm adopted and thinking about searching for my biological parents. Is this something I should do now? Is the time right? Will I find them? Will they be receptive? [I]

- My sister committed suicide two years ago. Why did she do it? How is she? Does she regret it? What has she done since then? Does she know we miss her? [PR]

- Will you please connect with my soul and find out what my purpose for being here is? [PR]

- What was my past-life relationship with the woman currently in my life? It feels like we have some unfinished business from sometime way back when, and I want to check and see if it's true. [PR]

- Six weeks ago the doctor told me I had a heart problem. Is this accurate? What should I do about it? [PR/I]

- I'm obsessed with a man in my life. We broke up several years ago and I still can't get him off my mind. What should I do to resolve this? [PR]

- Should I move to Texas? Should I pay for my young adult children to move there with me? Will my new job work out? How long will it take to sell my house? [I]

- What can I do about the low self-esteem I've had all my life? What's the cause of it? [PR]

- I feel as if I have psychic abilities, but I have a great fear of them. Where does this come from and what can I do about it? Should I pursue developing my psychic abilities? [PR]

- I have a disc problem in my lower back that I have worked on for several years with only minor relief. What should I do to heal it? [PR/I]

- I have had a connection with angels since I was a small child. What is this all about? [PR]

Psychic Abilities

- I am six months pregnant and I would like to know about the soul of my baby. Also, what is the sex of my child and how will my labor and delivery go? [PR]

- What was the reason for my car accident seven years ago? I still suffer a lot of pain from it. What can I do to heal myself? [PR/I]

As you can see, the questions are as varied as the people who ask them.

Using Intuition in Conjunction with Psychic Work

Although being psychic and intuitive are two different things, that doesn't mean intuition can't be enormously helpful in psychic work. It can be invaluable in discerning which incoming information is accurate and which isn't. It can also aid with interpreting pictures and visions.

For example, a client comes to a psychic asking if her husband is having an affair. The clairvoyant may get an image of a brunette sitting behind a receptionist's desk. A man then comes into the picture, and the psychic can see the two people flirting with each other. If the psychic hasn't learned to check out the picture with her intuition, she might just assume that the answer is yes, the man is having an affair with the receptionist in his office. But if the psychic consults the inner voice and asks if this picture means the man

71

is having an affair, the intuition may say, "*no, just flirting*" or "*yes, he's having an affair.*" The psychic could then check her intuition to see if the affair is actually with the receptionist in his office or symbolic of something else and, depending upon the answer (which can possibly even be affected by whether or not the client is meant to know the truth), the intuition will answer yes or no, or perhaps nothing will come. So the picture itself comes from the psychic realm, but the interpretation is aided by intuition.

Here's another example using clairaudience: A client asks when he is going to get a raise. The clairaudient hears the word "*springtime.*" Without having checked it out intuitively, the psychic might jump in and say, "You'll get a raise in the spring." But if he runs it by his intuition, this might happen: "Is spring accurate?" "*Yes.*" "Is it next spring?" "*No.*" "Spring in two years?" "*Yes.*" That's how psychic skill and intuition work in partnership.

Remember:

Clairvoyance is *seeing* pictures, visions, and images.

Clairaudience is *hearing* thoughts from different sources — the living, the dead, the spirit realm.

Clairsentience is *sensing* information.

Intuition is inner *knowing*.

Spirit Guides

Every one of us has at least one spirit guide who communicates to us through one or more of the psychic abilities we just discussed.

People often ask me why they can't see their guides and why their guides don't prevent bad things from happening in their lives. The "job" of our spirit guides is to help our soul stay on the path it chose this lifetime, and they communicate to our souls on a daily and nightly basis. Their foremost purpose is to guide and communicate with our soul, and that's why we aren't aware of them and why we can't readily see them.

Spirit guides are made up of energy and can appear to us in many ways, usually in a form similar to ours. We are receiving guidance from them all the time, whether we're aware of it or not. We get pictures in our heads, or thoughts come into our minds, and usually we think these are just our typical thoughts or pictures when they are actually guidance from the spirit realm. They also communicate to us through dreams, and through the sensing part of us, our clairsentience.

The movie *Always* does a great job of depicting spirit guides. The angel instructs the pilot how to communicate with the man he's watching over, telling him to send thoughts to him. That's exactly how it works sometimes. As we develop our psychic abilities, we are able to *slowly* make conscious contact with our spirit guide or guides, and over time we can actually see and hear them on a regular basis.

In answer to the question about why they don't prevent bad things from happening to us, the fact is they have a higher, more detached perspective about our life experiences and don't interfere with the choices our soul has made. Very often, what seems like a bad experience at the time proves to be the perfect thing necessary to help us grow and evolve more quickly and create a life experience that is more satisfying and fulfilling.

If you've been trying to make contact with your guides but aren't feeling like you're having much success, just remember that they are there and have been there all along. This kind of communication takes time, so be patient. Let your intuition guide you. Ask to contact your guides in your own unique way.

Ask for guidance from your guides as you would ask a friend for guidance. Don't make it a formal prayer, or a prayer of any kind. Guides don't like it when you pray to them — they are friends to your soul, and they are not God, and not to be confused with God.

If you want or need help with major issues in your life, go directly to the Source, and pray to God. If you want daily guidance and companionship, talk to your guides — and you'll never walk alone.

Chapter 4

Living by a Still, Small Voice

*Growing spiritually can be like a roller coaster ride.
Take comfort in the knowledge that the way down
is only preparation for the way up.*

— Rabbi Nachman of Breslov

If there's something we want in our life, whatever it may be, we have to put out effort to get it. When we meet someone we're interested in, we communicate this to them in many different ways. We call them on the phone, send notes, cards, or e-mails. We go for walks together and share meals with them. We tell them we want to have a relationship with them and do whatever we can to cultivate it. We talk, we listen, we share, we get to know one another — and that's exactly how it is when we develop a relationship with our intuition.

A lot of people think God is too busy running the world to listen to their everyday thoughts, feelings, concerns, and fears;

many people have told me they don't want to bother Him/Her with their little problems and desires. I understand this way of thinking all too well because I used to think that way myself. I used to feel completely insignificant in the bigger scheme of things, and believed the only way I could ask for some of God's time was if I was dealing with a major problem or a life-altering decision. But then I discovered the presence of God within me, and realized we all have God within us, at every moment of our lives.

In her book *Lessons in Truth*, Emily Cady distinguishes a personal God (the God within us) and an impersonal God (the God of the world). Here's a story that illustrates the difference:

When I was young, I had a close personal relationship with my father. He of course thought of me as his child and knew what my needs and wants were. He also had a much larger capacity: He was a wealthy, powerful man who ran a very successful company with offices all over the country. When he went to work, he focused on worldly concerns and was able to take care of whatever needed tending to. At any given time throughout the day, however, no matter what challenge or problem he was tending to, if one of his kids called him on the phone, he always had time to listen to us.

That's very much how I think about God. There's the impersonal God who tends to the matters of the world and the personal God who is there for any of his children when we have a need for His/Her attention.

Hearing God's Voice

How do we get a dialogue going with our personal God? By talking. Talk while you're driving the car or riding your bike. Talk in the shower, in the garden, working around the house, walking the dog. Talk, knowing He/She is listening. Talk to Him/Her like you would to a best friend, a confidant, a loving parent, the source who created you and loves you unconditionally.

Your conversations with God don't have to be formal, or structured. Talk about your day, about your thoughts and feelings. Share who you are, and what your dreams are. Ask for advice if you need it. Talk things over. The part of the relationship we often call prayer is simply talking.

The other part of the conversation is just like any other: Listen. Give God time to respond. Don't expect a deep thundering voice from on high. Listen for anything, as attentive as you can be.

Once, when I was going through a particularly difficult time, I went to my minister and told him that I had been talking to God, but God wasn't answering me. He told me that God whispers quietly — He doesn't shout — and when we're upset and seeking God's direction, it's our job to quiet ourselves so we can hear God's response.

At that time, I didn't like that one bit. I wanted God to shout answers to me from the rooftops, or give them to me in writing, preferably on stone tablets like the ones Moses received. "Stop making this so difficult," I told God one day. "I need some answers and I need them now. I don't want to have to calm myself down and wait to hear your soft, gentle voice. I want it loud and clear. Shout it out to me, God!" But it didn't do any good. The voice still spoke softly.

As much as we might wish for God to speak in a loud, commanding voice, He/She doesn't. When we ask for help, we have to calm ourselves down enough to hear the still, small voice inside.

So how do we hear the still, small voice? There are a few different ways. The first and most important way is to get in the habit of tuning into the voice within your gut rather than the one in your head. Remember the Albert Einstein quote that opened this book: "The intuitive mind is a sacred gift and the rational mind is a faithful servant. We have created a society that honors the servant and has forgotten the gift." We've somehow gotten things turned around. We need to go to our intuition for guidance and then to our brilliant, creative minds for support and implementation.

Talk to your inner wisdom throughout the day, and ask for guidance whenever you need it. Turn off the radio and television once in a while so that you regularly have periods of silence. Take time away from people, so you can focus within at times. Put your focus deep within, in the middle of your body. Ask your divine intelligence if it's in there, and slowly but surely you'll feel a subtle inner response. Connecting with your intuition, your divine intelligence, may be a long process, and you have to trust the timing of it. Be patient. It probably won't happen as fast as you want it to, but just keep reminding yourself that it's well worth whatever time is required. Keep in mind, when trying to discern the different voices inside, that intuition does not give emotional responses. Whenever you get a feeling to do something and it has an emotion attached to it — like fear, anger, shame, or guilt — that is definitely not intuition.

Start Small

When you're just starting to develop this awareness, ask for help with the little things. Let's say you have errands to run. You need to get to the post office, drugstore, grocery store, pet shop, and dry cleaners. Ask the voice within which things you should do first. When you go to make a purchase, ask if this is a good idea. When you want to get hold of someone, ask divine guidance to let you know when it would be good to call. Build up a trust with it. Let it prove itself to you. Just as you would do with any new relationship, take baby steps at first to get to know this voice within you.

I suggest to my students that they keep a little notebook in their pocket or purse and jot down the answers and guidance that they feel they're getting throughout the day. Keeping track like this helps you stay connected to the still, small voice within. It also helps you become conscious of just how much this inner guidance is already working with you.

Check In Regularly

Before crawling out of bed in the morning, ask God if there's anything you need to know for that day or if there's anything He/She wants you to do. Then let yourself relax, and just lie there for a while in that hazy place between sleep and wakefulness, and simply focus on your inner self before you jump out of bed and get into your head. Ideas will pop in as you lie there; you'll get an inspiration to do something or perhaps call someone. Sometimes nothing comes, which means you can plan your day the way you want to. On your way to work or school, ask that you be guided throughout the day for your highest good.

Until your mind learns to trust your intuition, it will probably try to run some kind of interference throughout each of these exercises. Gently remind it to relax. Reassure your mind that it's still very important to you and that you're very grateful for how well it works. Tell it you'll include it in all affairs of the day — *after* the Universe has given you its suggestions.

As you move through your day, continue to check in. You can think of it as a walkie talkie, if you wish: you're on one end and God's on the other, a source that knows all and sees all. After a while you'll realize that you've discovered a whole new way of doing things. It makes your life simpler, easier, and far more satisfying.

On those mornings that you get a late start and don't have time to lie in bed and *listen,* just "plug yourself in" whenever you become aware of it. It's never too late to do the check-in for the day.

Keep a God Journal

One of my favorite suggestions is to keep a "God Journal." Get a blank journal that is extra special to use for writing letters to God. I write all my concerns, thoughts, feelings, questions, needs, and wants in there. It's a good way to get focused and also to connect with God in a different way.

Sometimes I take my journal out to lunch with me and pretend I'm having lunch with God. I'll jot down a question and then write out the message I get back from my inner voice. I ask all kinds of questions. Sometimes I get an answer and sometimes I don't, but I always feel plugged into God when lunch is over. That feeling of inner calmness permeates my whole being.

Sit in the Presence of God

Another way to access God's voice is through meditation, or what I call "sitting in the presence of God." There's been so much written about meditation over the years that many of us have become completely intimidated by the mere thought of it. But there's no need to be. Meditation is the simple act of listening, something we all know how to do. The only difference between meditation and the listening we usually do is just that in meditation we're listening to a silent voice rather than a noisy one. Once you experience how loving your inner voice can be, and how much it wants to help you, you'll realize that meditation is actually a wonderful gift, not a discipline or punishment. We can usually get all the guidance we need through meditation.

It just takes practice. Let's try a simple guided meditation to get you started sitting in the presence of God. First we'll do a clearing exercise, which is very important to do every day. (If you're worried about time, relax, it takes all of twenty seconds.)

Close your eyes and take a nice deep breath from your solar plexus, not a shallow one from your chest. Blow it out. Now take another one and blow it out. One more time. Blow it out. Now ask the Universe to please clear you.

"Please clear my mind. Please clear my mind." Now, continue to take these relaxing breaths and ask the Universe to please clear your body. "Please clear my body." Next, ask it to please clear your soul. "Please clear my soul." If you need to do it again, then do it. The point of this is to get rid of the day's "stuff" so that you can go into that secret place without being distracted by the day or by thoughts of other people.

Now you're ready for the meditation. Sit wherever you're comfortable, take everything off of your lap, uncross your legs and arms, take a couple more relaxing breaths, relax your shoulders and forehead, and with your eyes closed (hard to do that and read a book, I know!) focus on your solar plexus. Use your imagination and visualize a white light, similar to a flame on a candle. Just sit for a while and focus on it.

Now imagine that the light is growing with each breath you take. Imagine it has a light, playful, creative, loving feeling to it as you focus on it, and continue to see the light growing and growing, until it becomes so big it envelops your whole being. Just let yourself be in this presence, and whenever your mind starts to wander, bring it right back to focusing on the light within you and around you. Every living creature has this light within itself, so you're not creating something that isn't there. After a while, when you come into this secret place, you'll automatically see the light and *know* it's for real. Keep your focus on the light, and, at some point, ask yourself if you sense a *voice* within the light. If so, listen to what it has to say to you.

When you feel ready to come back to your normal consciousness, take another deep breath to connect back with your body, count to three, and open your eyes. You'll be relaxed and feel a sense of calm, your mind will be clear headed, and you'll be ready to go back into your life.

You have just (a) cleared yourself of other people's energy that you picked up throughout the day, (b) connected to your Higher Self by focusing on the white light and the voice within the light, and (c) felt the presence of the source that created you. You sat in the presence of God.

As you get to know the energy inside, it will express itself in different ways. When I first started seeing the energy of my Higher Self, I saw a beautiful white energy that looked like a sword. When I asked why it looked like a sword, the answer I got was that it was my protector. As I continued to go within, the sword got bigger and eventually encircled me. Since then, the sword has changed into other images. At times I've seen it as a male figure, and at other times a female figure. Sometimes the energy expresses itself in beautiful colors.

You never know what you're going to see when you shut the world out and go into your sacred space: It's always changing and expressing itself in different ways. Over time, your communications with this energy will become stronger. You will get clear answers and guidance for your life. You will feel a oneness with God that you never thought possible.

If you keep doing this meditation, your perception of life will even change, and slowly you'll become emotionally detached from the life experiences your soul chose to have. You'll see the wisdom of your life lessons and have a different understanding of yourself and of God. That deep loneliness inside dissolves when we realize we have constant companionship within us, and the pieces of life fall into place like a jigsaw puzzle.

This is what Jesus meant when he said, "The kingdom of heaven is within." When we discover the *real* God, who permeates every cell of our being and who loves us unconditionally no matter what, something inside us begins to heal. And it continues to heal as we work at this relationship. We realize that the source that created us wants only the best for us, and we feel a partnership with this presence that we've yearned for all our lives.

For the rest of our lives, we walk hand in hand with this presence, always knowing that no matter what happens to us during our lifetimes on Earth, we're here for our highest good and our experiences are providing us with invaluable life lessons.

Hearing God in a Crisis

Nobody told us life on Earth was going to be easy. When our souls were in the planning stages of our life, we knew that coming here was going to be stressful and sometimes challenging, but we didn't look at these things as reasons not to come.* Stress is one of our key challenges in life, and we can choose how we

---

* See my book *Echoes of the Soul* for further explanation.

react to it: We can simply succumb to it, believing it's inevitable and can't be changed, or we can see it as an opportunity for growth, and find ways to transmute it into acceptance — and even serenity.

One of the hardest things to do when you're feeling stressed is to hear the voice of your intuition. You have to find ways to calm yourself down. Probably the hardest part of dealing with any crisis is figuring out how to let go of stress and tension, and how to slow down. Many of us have used alcohol, drugs, or food to help us do that. Now we've got another way.

One of the extra perks of living by your intuition is that you know where to go to get calm when you need to. No matter how stressed you might be, if you can discipline yourself to go to that sacred space inside, you can calm yourself down. Here are some steps you can take to help the process along:

1. If there are other people involved in your stressful situation, tell them you need a time out, and then get up and take yourself out of the environment.

2. Go outside or find some other quiet place if you can. If not, just start walking and while you're walking, ask the Universe to clear your body, mind, and soul.

3. Find a place where you can sit down, relax for a moment, and close your eyes. Do some deep breathing and focus on the white light within you. Just ask

the presence of God to surround and protect you
while you go through this stressful time.

4. Calmly ask your inner voice for guidance. Sit still a
moment and listen to what comes to you.

Remember, you can meditate anywhere — on the beach,
riding the bus, sitting at your desk, riding the train or plane, lying
in the sun, taking a five-minute cat nap. Just put your sunglasses
on and no one will know what you're doing!

The key to living life intuitively lies in always taking the time
to do what you need to do to stay plugged into your source. Just
keep it simple: Ask, listen, trust, and do. You won't regret it.

The Dark Night of the Soul

Once you get accustomed to hearing that inner voice of your
Higher Self, once you have found your connection to God, there's
nothing worse than going through a dark night of the soul or, as
I call it, *the dreaded silence.* In spite of everything we have learned,
in spite of all our attempts to reconnect, we find ourselves in a
place where there is no inner talking, no nudging, no knowing,
no nothing! Just silence. It's a lonely, empty, despairing place, but
it seems as if nearly everyone on a spiritual path goes through it
at some time.

Living by your inner voice is like walking through life with your best friend in your pocket. You never feel alone or insignificant. When you come to rely on your inner knowing for everything, for all your decisions and direction, and you continually get answers that show you how much this Higher Self loves you, you feel an inner knowing that your presence here on Earth is part of a much bigger picture, and your life and your work are valuable and essential.

And so, when you experience a dark night of the soul and all you can feel is silence and disconnection, your first tendency will be to question everything you have ever learned, everything in your reality. You'll wonder if you've been foolish to depend on this higher voice. You'll wonder if it was all real or just imagined. You'll doubt your specialness because, after all, if you were so special why would God abandon you?

The experience can definitely feel like you're sitting in the dark — it's as if you're feeling in the dark about everything in your life, and there is no life line nearby in case you start to drown. It's awful, but I promise you, it will pass. Just remember: you've done nothing wrong and you're not being punished. Don't try figuring it out because the mind can go on endlessly, and it doesn't help. No amount of begging for the voice to talk to you will get it back. It's as if someone pushed the mute button, and you just have to wait for them to come back and turn the volume back on.

I've been through some pretty tough dark nights of the soul and they always feel like they'll last forever, but they don't. All you need to do is just keep talking to God, whether you can feel an answer or not, and make up a big sign to hang nearby that says THIS TOO SHALL PASS.

Much has been written to try to explain dark nights of the soul, but I find that I always go back to what my mom told me: These are the times that test our faith, and when we come out of them, our faith will be much stronger. We will feel closer than ever to God, and we will appreciate the guidance we receive all the more. This has certainly been true for me.

Chapter 5

Rocking the Boat

*Trusting our intuition often
saves us from disaster.*

— Anne Wilson Schaef

I've always found it easier to live intuitively during the times
when I've been single. Then I don't have to explain to a partner that God's been talking to me. Our partners can feel threat-
ened when we live by the guidance of the voice within. It can
create problems, especially if our partners are controlling ones, or
are still living by the mind alone. They won't understand what
you're talking about or why you'd want to live this way.

People not on this path may try to change you. They'll tell
you they want you to be "normal" like everybody else. They won't
want you to take the time to listen to your inner voice; they'll
want you to make decisions quickly, like they do. They'll say
things like "join the real world," or tell you that you're being

weird, or that it's irresponsible to live like this. Having walked in their shoes, you can understand their resistance, but you can't keep wavering back and forth between pleasing others or following the voice within. There are times when you have to choose.

Following the Inner Voice

Here's what happened to me not too long ago when I followed the inner voice rather than the crowd:

A few years ago, my fiancé asked me if I would be interested in renting a fifty-foot houseboat in the Florida Keys for a week with him, his two sisters, and their husbands. I told him I needed to meditate on it, and when I asked my inner voice about it I got a strange feeling. Not a yes or no, just a strange feeling. I asked for a clearer answer every day for a week, but all I got was the same odd feeling, with no clarity. It was something my boyfriend really wanted to do, and so I eventually said yes. Whenever we got together with his family to plan the trip, that same vague, weird feeling would come up in my stomach, but since I never got a clear yes or no, I passed it off as anxiety about being in close quarters with five other people for seven days.

A week before we were to leave, my inner voice finally spoke clearly and told me that I wasn't supposed to go on the trip. Even though I had been expecting that the voice might tell me that, I still couldn't believe it was happening. I panicked at the thought of having to tell my fiancé that I wasn't going on the trip, and trying to explain it to his family. He had already shelled out the money for my airfare and my space on the boat, and here I was about to tell him I wasn't going to go, based only upon a vague feeling and a quiet inner prompting.

I kept asking my intuition if it was sure this was the right thing to do, and I would get a clear *yes* every time. But when I asked why, I got nothing. I spent one whole afternoon crying because I didn't think I had the courage to tell him I wasn't going. This was definitely one of those times when I wondered if I should just forego this whole intuition business and do what others expected of me.

Needless to say, Mike wasn't very happy when I told him. Over the course of the next week, he asked me several times if I would change my mind, and I kept telling him it wasn't my *mind* that needed changing. Of course that wasn't easy for him to understand.

The morning they left for the trip, I went into meditation and again asked what this was all about. What I heard was that this had happened exactly as it was supposed to, because if I had said no in the beginning, Mike wouldn't have gone — and a good vacation was long overdue for him, something he really needed. When I asked about me, I heard that I had to trust that there was a divine plan at work and to just watch how the week progressed.

I was in the last stages of writing *Echoes of the Soul* at the time, but I had been blocked for weeks, unable to get the two final chapters written to meet the deadline. I had hoped to get it finished before the trip but I hadn't gotten anywhere. Every day that Mike was gone, I was told in my morning quiet time to spend the day in silence, which meant no radios, TV, or phones. Throughout each day they were gone, creative ideas about the book kept coming, and I finished the entire manuscript the night before he got home. Once again the wisdom of the Universe had worked through me to meet my deadline and keep the book on schedule.

When I asked Mike if he would have gone if I'd initially said no, he said he definitely wouldn't have, but he was really glad he went because he ended up having a great time. The unexpected bonus from the Universe was that three months later his kids called from New York and asked if he'd come out for a visit, and he was able to use the unused airline ticket he had bought for me. The bottom line is that I trusted my intuition and acted upon it, even though it was difficult, and it worked for me again, even though I didn't know *why* at the time.

To Thine Own Self Be True

One of the most challenging slogans to live by that I came across in recovery is "To Thine Own Self Be True." Today I understand how important being true to ourselves is when it comes to fulfilling the destiny we come here to experience. Yes, it's very difficult to live by — there's a world full of people we want love and acceptance from, and sometimes we have to sacrifice that to be true to ourselves and live by our internal voice. Whether our intuition is telling us to say *no* to something our friends or family are in favor of, or *yes* to things they're warning us to stay away from, going with our own intuition is always for the best in the end. Here are some examples of some of the challenges we face when we make a commitment to follow our intuition:

- You've made plans with someone to go shopping or to the movies or on a date, but when the day arrives you get a strong feeling not to go.

- You get a job transfer and have a strong feeling not to go where the company wants to send you.

- You get two job offers and your family and friends — and your intellect — say to go with the job that pays better and has greater benefits, but your inner voice tells you to take the other job.

- You and your spouse agreed when you married to have two children, but your inner voice is strongly nudging you not to have the second child, or to have a third.

- You're engaged to someone, but whenever you think about making wedding plans, you get a feeling not to. (I had a friend who had a strong feeling not to marry her fiancé, but she went ahead with the plans anyway. When I asked her why she was going against everything that told her not to, she said she really wanted to wear the wedding dress she had bought and she didn't want to devastate her boyfriend by calling off the wedding. They've now been married a little over a year and she says every day has been hell!)

• You've got all kinds of financial challenges and your financial advisor is suggesting you get a second job to pay off your high debt. Your intuition, on the other hand, is suggesting bankruptcy and taking some time off.

• Your parents want you to go to a certain college but you get a strong feeling to go somewhere else.

• Your boyfriend wants you to move in with him but you get a strong feeling not to.

• You're expected to continue on in the family business and you get a strong pull in another direction.

• Your husband is about to retire and wants to move somewhere else, but you have a feeling you need to stay where you are.

• All your friends are buying motorcycles — you really want to be an accepted part of the crowd, and you even have the money to make the purchase, but your inner voice says not to.

• Society and your family say because you're a woman, you're expected to be a wife and a mother, but your inner voice says there's a different plan for you.

• All of your friends are going to a party, but you get a feeling to stay home.

• You're looking for property to buy and you think you've found something. You ask the realtor to go with you to the site three or four times before you sign the papers, but the day you're supposed to make the purchase you get a loud and clear voice that says no way.

• You and a dear friend have planned for over a year to open a business together, but as the day approaches to apply for the loan, your inner voice says *wait*.

• You go to the doctor and she orders a battery of tests that your inner voice says are not necessary.

• Your literary agent calls to tell you he finally sold your manuscript to a wonderful publishing house but your inner voice has a mixed reaction of good and bad feelings.

Situations like these come up for us throughout our lives, and the challenge is always whether we're going to be true to our friend, our family members, the realtor, the doctor, our minds, or our inner voice. It's important to remember that things are not always as they appear, and that we rarely can see the whole picture in any given situation. Sometimes when the inner voice says *no*, it's not even about us. It could be about other people in our life. For example, if your inner voice tells you not to buy what seems to be the perfect piece of property, maybe it's because it's really intended for someone else.

Maybe the reason your intuition tells you your husband shouldn't retire is not because something bad will happen if he does but because his company is about to offer him a big raise to stick around for a few more years. The inner voice that warns you not to marry your fiancé may not be telling you you shouldn't have been engaged to him — who knows, you two might be working out some karma from a past life — but just that you're really supposed to *marry* someone else.

I know living this way of life can be difficult if the people in your life aren't walking the same path as you are — and it can be especially difficult if they don't understand the path you have chosen — but that's no reason not to do what your inner guidance tells you to do. You're here to fulfill *your* purpose for being here. This is about *your* journey, *your* soul's development, and *your* relationship with your creator.

Controllers

Years ago, after the breakup of a relationship, my therapist said, "Look what's happened to you — you've completely lost yourself." I was so far gone emotionally that I had no idea what she was talking about. She went on to explain that when we're being true to ourselves, we hear the guidance from our intuition and live our lives accordingly, but when we give our power to another person, we stop listening to our intuition. We look to the other person to direct and guide us, and after a while we forget who we are. Unfortunately, a lot of us allow this to happen because of our deep need to be loved and our fear of loneliness.

The man I had been involved with was a very controlling person who never honored the wisdom of intuition. He would tell me to "get real," and say that the way I was trying to live was stupid and foolish. In every situation, he'd tell me what to do, what to wear, where I could and couldn't go, what he wanted my career to be, what to say to his friends and his family, and how to act. If I seemed the least bit ungrateful, he would pull his "look at all I've done for you" routine, and I would be shamed back into my dependence on him. We were quite the pair. He was king controller and I was queen co-dependent. There was a part of me that resisted constantly, and another part of me that didn't think I could survive without him. I felt constantly torn between listening to my inner wisdom and listening to this man I was so addicted to.

Breaking away from that relationship took many years but it was worth every painful step. As I said earlier, we can't be true to our inner voice and to the voices of the world at the same time. That never works when we're walking the spiritual path.

Co-dependents

Becoming more intuitive is particularly hard for people who feel they have no power, or who have given their power to someone else. If this describes you, I'm here to tell you that you have *all* the power you need right inside you, right now. If you've given your power away, you can always get it back — *but* you have to stop living for others and trying to please others. If this is a major issue for you, my best suggestion for a place to start making some changes is to read Melody Beattie's *Co-dependent No More*. Read it and get going on your own path.

When a co-dependent starts walking her own path, look out! There are all kinds of new challenges and opportunities for growth for *everyone* involved. The people in your life who are so used to having you there *for them* all the time aren't going to like it one bit. Just keep reminding yourself that you're here this lifetime to advance your soul's growth and development, and learning to listen to and live by your intuition is by far the greatest way to do this. You'll find that you'll never be in a situation too difficult for you to handle, and your intuition will show you how to deal with all the new challenges and opportunities that come your way.

If you decide you want to tell the significant people in your life what you're doing, I always suggest keeping it simple. Explain that you've changed the way you do things and that you're learning to listen to and live by your inner voice. Don't expect it to be easy. On my second date with the man who is now my fiancé, I told him that I talk to God about everything that goes on in my life and I live according to the guidance I get from within. When I asked him if he would have a problem with that, his response — which of course won my heart — was, "Aren't we all supposed to live like that?"

You don't have to apologize to the people in your life for what you're being led to do. Remember, they chose, on a soul level, to be in your life. God loves them as much as you do and has a plan in mind for them as well.

One of the perks of living from intuition is that after a while you'll start attracting people of like mind. Other people that live by their intuition will come into your life and you'll constantly feel affirmed that you're on the right track.

There's just one more thing to consider about rocking other people's boats: *it might be the best thing that ever happened to them.* Read the next chapter and see how it turned out for my ex-husband.

Chapter 6

The Universal Big Ben

*Intuition will tell the thinking mind
where to look next.*

— Jonas Salk

When you stop living by other people's voices and begin to get your guidance from the calm and clear voice of the Universe, you become aware of a magical flow at work with all the people you interact with. This is what I call universal timing. It reminds me of traffic. When everyone is honoring each other and paying attention to the signs, traffic flows. So it is with living your true path — you constantly find synchronicity and coincidences happening. You find yourself in the right place at the right time over and over again. I like to think of "the flow" as God's timing.

As mind boggling as it is to comprehend, the Universe has an awareness of everything that's going on and can guide us accordingly. The process is mysterious and magical, involving divine energy. There is a piece of God in each one of us, and because of that, we are all connected to each other. The divine part of us runs on divine timing. When we are plugged into that divine energy, we operate in the perfect flow of timing.

This story should illustrate my point:

A few years ago, I was trying to find my old friend Mary, who had edited my first book, *Hands that Heal*. I was finishing my second book at the time, and needed an editor. I called all the numbers I had for her and found out that she'd gotten married, moved, and had an unlisted number. I asked the Universe to please help me locate her. About a week later, on a Sunday morning, my inner voice told me to go to Lunds grocery store at noon. My logical mind jumped in and thought, "Noon on Sundays is a terrible time to go to Lunds. It's always so crowded then." But my inner voice got a little louder, *"Lunds, noon."* As much as I wanted to stay in my pajamas and take my time reading the Sunday paper, I got up and drove to the store at noon. When I walked into the store I felt a strong inner nudge to go over to the dairy section. I had no need for any dairy items, I was simply following my inner prompting. I headed over there and ran right into Mary. She said she'd been getting an inner nudge to call me for about a week but hadn't gotten around to it, which affirmed to me that the Universe had been trying to hook us up.

It's obvious to me from so many experiences like this that I've had that there is a universal timing that knows everything. It knows if you're about to face a health challenge, if an unexpected guest will be visiting for a month, if your car is going to break down, if a death is going to occur in your life, if your pet is about to be sick, if your nephew is going to need to spend some quality time with you, if you're going to win the lottery, if your spouse is going to ask for a divorce, how the weather's going to be for your special function, if you're going to write a bestseller, if and where you're going on vacation, if you're going to fall in love and with whom, if you're going to get a raise, if you're going to lose your job, if you're moving, if you're dying, if you're going to patch things up with an old friend. It knows the right timing for phone calls and errands. If you're having a heated discussion, it will guide you when to speak and when to be quiet. It will tell you when to plant your garden and when not to. We'd all do well to ignore the experts and go with the Universe instead. And the more we are in touch with our own intuitive voice, the more "in the flow" we will be.

I recommend that you check in with your intuition several times a day, just to get in sync with timing.

Several years ago when it seemed like perfect timing to plant my garden, my inner voice kept telling me *no*. I really struggled with whether or not to listen to it. All my neighbors were planting their gardens and I kept wondering why it was okay for them but not for me. As spring progressed into summer, we had a terrible drought and all my neighbors lost the beautiful flowers they had planted that spring. They tried watering them but after a while the city asked people to conserve water by not watering their yards. I walked around all summer shaking my head in disbelief. I almost overrode its wisdom, but once again my intuition knew what was coming.

By tuning into "the Big Ben of the Universe," you'll also know when to get to the post office, grocery store, bank, movie theater, bus stop, prescription counter, dry cleaners, restaurant, and gas station when there's no waiting, no line. It's really very practical.

Yesterday at the grocery store the woman in front of me asked the clerk when they were going to be getting in more shrimp. After checking with the butcher, the clerk told her they would be unloading that shipment in about an hour. The lady asked if they could please unload it now so she wouldn't have to come back, but the clerk said no, they had to do things in a certain order and she would just have to come back in an hour!

We've all been there. I would bet you she'd gotten an intuitive nudge just before she left for the store, telling her not to go just then, and she ignored it because her head said this was the best or most convenient time to go.

Divine timing can be helpful in so many ways. Maybe your inner voice is telling you to wait to go to the store because the item you want is about to go on sale. Maybe you're headed out to an appointment but instead of leaving you get a feeling to wait for a few minutes. Heed that feeling! The Universe knows better than you do! Perhaps there's a three-mile traffic jam but it's about to clear; maybe the Universe is trying to prevent you from being in an accident; maybe the person you're meeting is just about to call to cancel, and by listening to the voice you'll save yourself the hour in the car.

A Life-Changing Book

Here's a good illustration of the power of divine timing. In 1986, I was teaching a psychic development class, and my students were all abuzz about a great new book called *Living in the Light* by Shakti Gawain. Every week when the class met, at least two or three different people would talk about how the book was changing their life. For a while, it seemed like everywhere I went, people were talking about this book and asking if I had read it.

Whenever I would think about getting it, however, my inner voice always said "*wait,*" so as embarrassing as it was to admit to people that I wasn't reading this hot new book, I just kept waiting for my inner guidance to say "*now.*"

In the summer of the following year, three different people called *on the same day* to say they'd felt led to call and tell me to read *Living in the Light*. So I went inside and asked God if the timing was right yet, and I got a resounding "*yes.*"

As I read through chapter after chapter, I felt like a starved animal who was finally being fed. I didn't want to put the book down. The book completely validated my inner voice, and helped the intuitive part of me to awaken in a way I had never known before. It didn't treat my intuition as something flaky or off the wall; it allowed me to recognize the sweet, subtle, loving voice within me as something very sacred and holy — as the Bible says, "the secret place of the most high." As I read each chapter, I felt as if I was finding a freedom within me that had been locked away for a long time, the freedom to be myself, and to be true to myself.

As wonderful as it was, it also created a huge conflict in my life. I was having problems in my marriage, but I had been determined to make it work. I had had the same dream everyone else seemed to have: a loving partner, a happy marriage, and a house with a white picket fence. But the more I read the book, the clearer I got about how unhappy I was and how much I was blocking myself from seeing the truth about the marriage.

I saw how afraid I had been to hear any divine guidance about our relationship. I was so afraid that God was going to tell me to get out of it that I limited my conversations with him to exclude anything about my marriage. I saw that in order to feel whole I needed to open myself up to inner guidance for all areas of my life, not just the safe ones. I started asking for direction about what to do with my marriage.

Daily, my inner voice talked to me about letting go of the marriage and moving on. It was difficult. I didn't like what I was hearing, but it always felt right. When I thought about leaving, I felt an inner peacefulness that I didn't feel when I thought about staying. I found myself arguing with divine guidance. All the *yeah, buts* kicked in. "Yeah, but how will I support myself financially?" "Yeah, but how will my husband handle this?" "Yeah, but what about our dreams and goals? What will our families say?" "Yeah, but what about all the therapy we've done?" "Yeah, but what about the dog?" I may not have always gotten clear answers to my questions, but I always felt an undeniable sense of inner calm when I thought about separating.

Within a week after I finished the book, I could no longer deny what my inner guidance was repeatedly saying, so I took several deep breaths, did the best I could do to clear myself, and told my husband it was time to let go of the marriage. The next few days were very emotional for both of us and, as my husband was packing some things to go and stay with friends of ours, my inner voice told me to get him a copy of *Living in the Light,* which I did.

About a week later, much to my surprise, he came by the house to say that the book had dramatically changed his perspective on things as well. He told me he felt guided to move to California to take some classes from Shakti Gawain. It felt so right to both of us that we had a huge garage sale and sold as much as we could so he would have the money to pursue his new dream.

Because we were both completely honest with each other, and both doing our best to live by divine guidance, we both had the sense that we were on the right track, and our divorce was friendly and we remained supportive of each other as we grew in different directions. My ex-husband not only met Shakti Gawain but married her, and they're now traveling and teaching together.

By listening to divine guidance, everyone ends up in the right place at the right time. I share this story because it shows many of the points I'm trying to make in this chapter:

1. Divine timing naturally occurs when we follow our intuition, whether we can understand it logically or not.

2. When we live according to divine guidance and not according to the voices of the world, all the right pieces fall into place.

3. Trust that God loves our loved ones as much as we do and has a plan for them as well. (I almost stayed in the marriage because I was concerned about my husband.)

4. In spite of how hard change is, when we're being divinely guided, we get courage from within to go through it. The Universe never hands us problems or challenges greater than we can handle.

Universal Will versus Our Will

How are we supposed to know if it's God's will guiding us or our own? I grappled with that question for a few decades! The way it was finally explained to me that made sense is that when it's Gods will, Universal will, or part of the divine plan (take your pick), God puts the desire in our hearts and then the Universe backs it up energetically. Let me explain in more detail:

We all know what desire feels like because we have desires that come and go all the time, but the key to recognizing whether it's God's will and desire or our will and desire is in the *consistency* of that desire. If it's God's will, He/She plants the seed in our hearts and the desire that grows from it will remain consistent. If, on the other hand, it's our desire or will for something, we'll want it at some times but not at other times. The desire will come and go — it's not consistent.

The word *desire* itself triggers a lot of negative thoughts associated with sin and society's restrictions, and feelings such as guilt and shame. We all have within us what I call universal desires as well as physical or sexual desires. Universal desires are a result of God's will. It's important to be able to distinguish God's will from your own. One sure way to tell the difference is that God's will doesn't go away.

Let's say you have a desire to buy a Harley Davidson (yes, this applies to women readers, as well as men). All your friends have one and you think it would be so cool to have one, too. You look in the paper and get more excited, but there's a funny little feeling in your gut about the whole idea. Every time you go to call the bank about applying for a loan, you can't seem to make the phone call, and you find other things to do instead. Over time, you find yourself thinking less and less about the bike. The reasoning part of your mind takes over and you put the idea of buying a Harley on the back burner. You'll reconsider later; maybe you'll wait until you retire. In that scenario, your desire was strong in the beginning but because it wasn't divinely inspired you slowly lost enthusiasm for the idea.

Now let's look at a situation that is similar, but is divinely inspired instead. You start to feel a deep desire in your heart to own and ride a Harley. You feel a desire to take a class, so you make a call and sign up for a class that just happens to fall on the only night of the week that you're free. You feel excited every time you think about your new endeavor, and yet there's a feeling of calmness and satisfaction as well. Classes go well and you gain a lot of confidence. When it comes time to shop for a bike, you meet the right people at the right time who sell you a bike for the right price. The pieces fall into place easily.

Your desire was constant. Although your logical mind might have argued from time to time, you never wavered and the entire experience continually felt right.

When the Universe has a plan for us and is trying to get us in touch with that plan, it creates a deep desire in us that we feel throughout our whole being. And there is always a universal energy that backs it up energetically, and we always end up in the right place at the right time, and the pieces of the plan fall into place easily.

One thing that always helps me when I'm not clear if I'm tapping into God's will or my own is to go ahead and ask God to remove the desire if it is *not* divinely guided. This has simplified my life in a great many ways.

Another clue to whether I'm feeling God's will or my own lies in the reasonability of it. My desire to spend a night frolicking with Jack Nicholson has remained constant for the last twenty years, but I'm pretty clear that this particular desire is not coming from God simply because it's not reasonable. All those poor people who stalk movie stars probably believe it's God telling them to do it, but if they could stand back and be objective about this desire, they'd see it's not reasonable. (Stalking someone has never proven to be a good way to start or to continue a relationship.)

Divine Timing

Sometimes an idea is divinely guided but the timing is a little off. Let's say your husband decides he's going to build a screened-in porch in the backyard. Several perennials need to be moved to another part of the yard in order to put the porch where you want it, but every time you tell yourself to get out there and get those things replanted, you don't feel any enthusiasm or energy to get it done. Even though he's busy drawing up plans to build it, you keep getting a feeling to wait. On the outside the plan looks like it's going to unfold this summer, but you continually forget to move the plants and then, when you do remember, there's still no internal push. You ask God if maybe you're just being lazy and get back an emphatic "*no.*" Listen to this guidance. Chances are, something else is going to take precedence over the screened porch and your husband won't get to it this summer. There's a reason this project is being put on hold. That's just the way the Universe works.

My friend Carl Luk-Sims, owner and editor of Namaste Publishing in London, recently told me that when it comes to putting his newspaper together, he and his wife Yin have learned that if an article isn't falling into place easily or if they're struggling with an idea, it's simply not meant to be. His words to me were, "If it ain't flowin', It ain't goin'."

The most profound experience I've ever had about divine timing goes back quite a few years. I was nineteen years old and in my second year of college, and when I went to sign up for classes that quarter, my inner voice kept saying it didn't matter what I took, because I wouldn't be finishing the quarter. I couldn't for the life of me figure out why that would be so. Halfway through the quarter, I found out that I was pregnant. It was a very difficult time in that everyone around me — boyfriend, parents, best friend, and minister — had very strong opinions about what would be best for me. I had to separate myself enough from all of them to hear the guidance from within.

My boyfriend was about to graduate from college, and he felt certain we could handle marriage and a baby — but I kept feeling internally that this was not the way it was supposed to go. From the moment I knew I was pregnant, I heard the inner voice tell me that I was meant to go full term with the baby — not have an abortion — and place him for adoption. I *knew* that was how it was supposed to go, and it was extremely difficult to tell all the concerned people around me what *felt* right to do. A many-sided conflict raged involving my inner voice, my logical mind, my desire to be a mother, and the feelings and opinions of so many others. I wanted to keep my baby and raise him myself, but no matter how much I tried to convince my inner voice, it always calmly said the best thing for the baby was to put him up for adoption.

Eighteen years later, I started asking my inner voice if I could begin searching for my son. Every time I asked, I heard "*no.*" For the next six years, whenever I asked, I always heard *no,* although when I would ask God if I was ever going to see my son again, I always heard "*yes, be patient.*" Because I know timing is so important for everyone concerned, I did not want to do this until I got a clear internal go-ahead.

One morning in June of 1992 I asked God as I was in my morning sleepy state if there was anything I needed to know or do that day, and my inner voice clearly said, "*Today you can begin looking for your son."* I bolted out of bed. I must have asked my intuition ten times if it really said I could start looking for my son, for those were words I had waited to hear for a long time. *Yes, yes, yes* — my inner wisdom kept saying *yes.*

As soon as I gained my composure, I asked the voice what I should do first. It told me to be patient, and that I would know sometime later that day.

Several hours later, my first client of the day came for a healing. I asked her what she needed healing for, and she said she was adopted and had just met her birth parents. She said that even though it was great to be reunited with them, she was going through a lot of emotional turmoil. I'm sure she could see my surprise as she told me the whole story of hiring an agency and how the process evolved. After our session I told her that my inner voice had just told me that morning that the timing was now right for me to start looking for my son, so as soon as she got home she called and gave me the agency's name and phone number.

The next day I called Post Adoption Search Team (P.A.S.T.) in San Jose, California. They said they'd send me some papers to fill out with all the necessary information. I just had to return the application along with a check for $300 to begin the search. Another $200 would be due when they found him. They said it would take between two to six weeks to find my baby!

I was thrilled beyond words, but a lot of fears came up as well: What if my son didn't want to meet me? What if he hated me?

What if I found out something terrible had happened to him — was I ready for anything that might happen? My other concern, since I wasn't working much at the time, was where I was going to get $300 by the end of the week.

I asked God to help me prepare mentally and emotionally for this whole experience, and the next morning I heard the words: "*Call Meg Bale.*" Meg was a social worker at Children's Home Society in St. Paul, whom I had met several years earlier when I helped my father find his biological mother. I called her that day and we talked for a long time on the phone. She was extremely helpful and recommended a couple of books she thought I should read to prepare for this new relationship.

By the end of the week, the papers arrived from P.A.S.T. There were also two checks in the mail: one for $75 from a client I had read months earlier who had never paid me and the other for $225 from some insurance policy whose company had gone defunct. It was unbelievable — I'd bought that policy years ago. Of all days for that check to arrive! I mailed back the forms and money and began reading everything I could to prepare.

Weeks passed and nothing happened. Fear crept in from time to time, and my inner voice always told me that everything was fine. Doreen, the woman conducting the search, told me they were having a tough time locating my son, but they hadn't given up. She said it was a matter of days.

Friday morning, August 10th, I had to put my dog to sleep, which was a very emotional experience for me. I was sitting in my office crying when the phone rang. I was going to let the answering machine get the call, but my inner voice literally shouted to me to answer it. It was Doreen. She called to say she didn't know where he was yet, but she knew his name and physical characteristics. I was disappointed that we still didn't know where he was, but I realized I needed each step of this experience to prepare mentally and emotionally to meet him. It could potentially be a life-changing event, and everything had to be right for all concerned.

Two more months passed. On Friday, October 30th, I got a call from Doreen, and this time she told me she had found my son in Nebraska. She gave me his phone number and coached me on what to say. I was ecstatic. Finally, twenty-four years after placing my baby for adoption, I knew his name and where he lived. I wanted to call him right away, but my inner voice said loudly, "*tomorrow morning.*" Tomorrow! Why not today? I asked, and all I heard was, "*call tomorrow morning.*"

As much as I wanted to pretend I didn't hear those words, I knew it was best to trust them, so I very impatiently waited until the next morning. I looked back over the four months it took to find him and realized that I needed every day of those four months to prepare myself for the possibility of having my son in my life. I had read the books and talked to the experts, and I felt ready.

The next morning I called my son and introduced myself. We ended up talking for an hour on the phone and we've had a very positive relationship ever since. When I told him that I'd gotten his name and number the day before but that something had told me to wait until the next day, he said he'd been home in bed from food poisoning and was really glad I'd waited to call.

One more bit of divine timing was involved: When I told him I'd started the search in June, he told me that in June he'd told his girlfriend that if they went to California (where he was born) for a friend's wedding, he was going to start looking for his biological mom.

I have an image that there is a huge invisible "Big Ben" clock out there in the cosmos, and the source that created us runs the entire Universe by this clock. The image is symbolic, not to be taken literally, but for some reason it represents — at least for me — what divine timing is, and how it works. When we check in daily with our source, our lives run by that same clock, and we will end up — *always* — in the right place at the right time. You may perhaps have a very different image that comes to your mind, or no image at all. But when you really understand that there is divine timing and divine order and you make a conscious decision to be a part of it, your life truly does become magical.

Chapter 7

One Day at a Time

Go into your room, and when you have shut your door, pray ... to your Father who is in the secret place.

— Jesus (Matthew 6:6)

L ately, it seems like I hear more and more people say they can't take much more stress. So many of us are stressed out so much of the time, overwhelmed with the demands of our lives. We've got so much to do — too much to do — from the time we get up until the time we finally lay our heads back down on that pillow. Every day seems to be packed with responsibilities, expectations, obligations, and unexpected challenges, and the thought of getting up the next day and doing it all over again drives alot of people to prescription drugs, alcohol, illegal drugs, or excessive or unhealthy food.

Living on Earth is challenging for all of us, but there are ways to make our journey here simpler and easier to handle. We can physically let go of stress through exercise, and we can let go of mental and emotional stress by learning to take deep breaths and *relax* whenever is necessary throughout our day. Regular periods of meditation and prayer are wonderful stress relievers, as well, And we have two other incredibly helpful tools available to us at all times. The first one is living by the help you get from your inner voice. The other is taking life one day at a time.

Everyone of us takes life for granted and thinks we'll be here forever, or at least for a long time to come. In my work as a healer, I am always amazed at how many of my older clients have the same story. All their adult lives they had looked forward to retirement. They'd saved all their extra money for their golden years. They had put off many of the things they'd wanted to do, thinking they'd do them when they retired — only to find themselves, within weeks of retiring, facing a serious health challenge. Now all that retirement money is going for medical bills, and they're scared and angry.

I also see many widows who come for healing for their grief because their husbands died shortly after retiring. It's always the same story: "We had so many plans, we scrimped and saved for the golden years." And then, so soon after retirement, their spouse died. They deferred their happiness, and now they're full of regrets.

I'm not saying we shouldn't plan for the future; I'm saying we can't depend upon the future to unfold according to our plans. Plan wisely, but don't put off until tomorrow those things you can do today. Live your life *now*.

I just did a reading for a woman who wanted to communicate with her deceased husband and find out how he's doing. When I connected with him, I discovered he wasn't very happy. He had died quite suddenly at fifty and was full of regret about the things he had hoped to experience with his wife in his later years. What a powerful reminder that we have only today.

Think about it. There's no guarantee you'll make it through the rest of this year, or even the remainder of this day. As much as we hate to hear that, it's the truth! That's why it's so important to live in the moment.

I'm certainly not saying anything new here. We've all heard it, but for most of us it hasn't changed the way we live our lives. We're heard it, but we haven't really *understood* it. When we finally do understand that we only have the time that's right in front of us, a great thing happens: a ton of stress lifts off our shoulders. Life is no longer overwhelming. We learn not only to cope but to starting having *fun*. Yes, fun.

Don't defer. Do it now. Do what you've been wanting to do, but have been putting off. Maybe it's something on this list. Take this list and start doing.

- I'll play with the kids — *today.*

- I'll take the time to read that novel — *now.*

- I'll eat healthier, because I want to feel better — *now.*

- I'll take that well deserved vacation — *now.*

- I'll call the people I love and tell them so — *today.*

- I'll take that class I've always wanted to — *today.*

- I'll start that project I keep fantasizing about — *today.*

- I'll write the letters I've been meaning to write — *today.*

- I'll make love — *today.*

- I'll visit the people dear to me — *now.*

- I'll go outside and smell the fresh air — *now.*

- I'll meditate, and pray, and check in with my intuition — *now.*

The Best Stress Buster

In the Lord's Prayer, Jesus instructs us to ask God to "give us this day our daily bread," which means to help us meet our daily emotional, mental, physical, and spiritual needs. He doesn't tell us to ask for our needs to be met for the week, or month, or year. He suggests we take it one day at a time.

When we ask our inner voice for help and guidance for the day, we are asking for our daily bread.

Whenever you find yourself feeling overwhelmed, ask yourself, "Have I stopped living in the now?" I'll bet the answer is *yes.* We all do it. We try to anticipate the things that will happen in the future so we can *feel* in control of our lives, but we almost always end up feeling overwhelmed and *out of* control. The best way to be in control of our lives is to stay in the present moment.

Listening to inner guidance helps us connect with the present. Look at your day planner and ask for guidance for the day — just today. Take your day in sections. First look at the morning hours and ask for guidance. Then look at the afternoon, and then the evening hours. At first it may seem awkward, but after a while it will become second nature. Just ask for guidance and stay in the present.

This doesn't mean that we're disregarding the future. A great thing happens when we focus on the present: It not only reduces stress and makes life a lot more enjoyable, it takes care of the future as well. When you ask for guidance for today, for example, you may also be told what you're going to talk about in a speech you're going to give in two weeks. You may be told to call a realtor today to start looking for property that you may not even purchase until retirement. Your inner voice knows the perfect timing for setting anything and everything in motion and when we focus only on today and leave the rest to our higher selves for guidance, we always get what we need — for today and for the future.

I know there are some of you still reacting to this with a few "yeah, buts." Let me try to put it in a different way: *You only have today,* so get creative with your time and enjoy it. *Now* is all you've got.

Back in the beginning of my spiritual journey, I was a secretary at an employment agency for recovering alcoholics. I was in the early stages of recovery myself, learning how to live a day at a time and also learning to trust God to meet my needs and wants.

The company was having financial problems, and our boss asked us if we would be willing to go without pay for a couple of pay periods while they got things straightened out. It was during the holiday season, and money was so tight that there was no choice but to live day to day.

My friend Millie Duncan ran the office and was quite a role model for anyone wanting to walk a spiritual path. She was always calm, and she kept telling us God would provide for our daily bread. Part of me wondered if she lived in "la-la land" and just didn't want to deal with reality, but another part of me witnessed the magic that took place in her life every day. One Friday, just before New Year's Eve, she invited one of the counselors and me out for lunch and told us we could have anything we wanted. We'd all existed on peanut butter sandwiches for so long that this was a real treat for us.

All through lunch, Millie talked to us about our fears of the future — none of us knew what was coming because of the way things were going at the company. She told us we really needed to focus on the present day, because there was no guarantee we'd still be here tomorrow. She said the *real* reason we were all going through this tough time was to learn that God would take care of us daily, and she told us she hoped we were learning it.

I can still remember watching her count out all the change she had in her coin purse to pay for our lunches. She said it didn't matter if she spent all of her money because tomorrow would be a new day with new possibilities.

I drove home that day wishing I could be more trusting like Millie. She was so sure God would provide all of her needs, and she was so disciplined about living in the now. She didn't seem to have much stress, in fact she brought a simple grace to every moment. When we got to work Monday, we found out Millie had passed away in her sleep sometime during the week-end. Her faith, her words, her wisdom, her life, and even her death taught me some of the most valuable lessons of my life, and I still live by them today: We do not have any guarantees that we will still be here tomorrow. If you simply ask the Universe for daily guidance and listen throughout the day to your internal voice, you will truly live your life to the fullest.

And then, when you do leave this lifetime, you will leave feeling completely fulfilled.

Chapter 8

Loving Signs from the Universe

I and my Father are one.

— Jesus (John 10:30)

Once we become aware of that still, small voice within, we not only connect with our inner guidance, we live our lives in harmony with the whole universe. The universe responds by supporting us in innumerable ways, and gives us countless "signs" that demonstrate that support.

Many people have a special "sign" that they believe is an indication of God's presence in their life. My mom has always said that whenever she asks God for a sign of his presence, a red cardinal appears. Nick Bunick tells us in the book *The Messengers* (written by Julia Ingram and G.W. Hardin) that the physical sign he has been given by the angels for the presence of God in his life is the appearance of the numbers 444. The signs are different for everyone.

When I was a little girl and asked God to give me a sign that he was really there, I heard the song of a mourning dove. Ever since then, I've often seen or heard mourning doves after I pray, and they continue to show up whenever I need an emotional lift, or some spiritual inspiration.

Dimes from God

Another manifestation of the presence of God in my life has to do with dimes.

Being self-employed has always had its challenges, the most obvious one being money. For many years now I haven't had a steady paycheck, and it's been difficult at times to budget my money to cover all my living and business expenses. Fortunately my intuition continually guides me about which bills to pay and when, and which bills to hold off on. Whenever I have an upcoming financial responsibility and can't see any way of paying it, I turn to my business partner and financial counselor — my inner guidance — for help, and a creative solution inevitably appears.

At some point years ago, I began to notice something very odd. Just when I'd be feeling panicked about money, a dime would appear in some strange place — and then some unexpected money would come my way. These weren't just "accountable" dimes, like the ones you find in the washing machine after putting your jeans in there or the stray ones you find by your nightstand where you keep your loose change. These would show up in truly outlandish places: on the steering wheel in my car, on top of a mayonnaise jar in the refrigerator, on top of a stack of towels in the linen closet, on the pillow in my bed, in the bed sheets by my feet, on top of the garbage can *after* the garbage was picked up, on a chair, in the bathtub, on my healing table, on top of the agitator in the washer, on top of the toilet seat cover, on top of my face cream jar, on a pair of socks in the drawer. One time there were five dimes in a perfect circle on the lawn as I mowed the grass! I'm not kidding. This dime thing was weird.

After it happened a few times, I began to realize this wasn't just a coincidence. I asked my inner voice what the dimes meant and it said they were God's way of saying that there is always enough money for whatever I need, and a way of showing that my prayers will be answered. I've come to call them my "God dimes."

For a long time, I kept all my little dime stories to myself, thinking they were so odd and quirky that people would just blow them off to chance or coincidence. I finally started telling some close friends and family members about it and, wouldn't you know it, dimes started appearing in their lives, too, always followed by money!

Take my friend Mary, for example. We met for dinner one night and had just been seated when I had a feeling to tell her about the dimes. I went through the whole story about how dimes would appear in odd places shortly after I had prayed for a solution to a financial challenge, and then these dimes were always followed by money from an unexpected source. Mary was skeptical.

I told her I knew it was hard to believe but it had happened so many times it was undeniable, at least for me. Right then the waiter came and took our orders and picked up our menus. Underneath Mary's menu was a dime, sitting exactly in the middle of her placemat. We asked the waiter if he had picked up his tips from the last person and he reassured us that he had.

Mary didn't know what to make of it — but from that day forward dimes started showing up in her life, too, always after she prayed for guidance with a financial situation.

Another friend of mine was completely skeptical about any mention of my "God dimes." Every time I'd tell him a dime story he'd just roll his eyes as if to say I was crazy. One day we were going for a drive and he asked me if I thought we should stop at the local casino. Casinos aren't exactly my favorite places, so I told him to check it out with his intuition.

We pulled into a restaurant to get a bite to eat and make our decision. Right after we sat down at the table and the waitress brought us each a glass of water, Tom burst out laughing and said, "Well, I'll be damned!" He told me to look at the bottom of my glass — and there was a dime, inside the glass, staring right at him whenever I took a drink of water! We did the rational thing and asked the waitress if she had put the dime in the glass, which, of course, she hadn't. She swore that the glass had been empty when she'd filled it. She said she certainly would have noticed or felt the dime in the bottom of the glass!

The most interesting thing about it all for me was that Tom didn't want to even talk about it. He was sure I'd somehow slipped the dime in there. He didn't want to open the door to the possibility of God's magic working in his life.

All of us have this choice every day — to open to the magic of our existence or to shut it out — but most people choose to ignore it because they don't want to appear gullible or "unrealistic." To me, this way of looking at things is a sad way to think and a disappointing way to live. So many of us let our fears — particularly our fear of being vulnerable — shut us off from discovering the magic of life.

We're Here for a Great Purpose

Something I've discovered in my fifty years is that life is full of disappointments, heartbreak, road blocks, and unexpected detours, but none of us is so fragile that we can't overcome these things. If we allow ourselves to heal from the painful experiences, we end up wiser and more open than before, able to appreciate the joy, the surprises, and the beauty of life more than ever.

Living on Earth is a challenge. That's undeniable. And if you're trying to live on a spiritual path and live by your inner voice, it can be especially challenging. The world's rules are different from Universal rules. A lot of the things that we see as so important here in the material realm are not that important at all in the bigger scheme of things. We so often get caught up in appearances and in what others think. We allow others to dictate our worth, and we judge our worth by external standards that simply aren't that important in the long run.

Families, friends, schools, businesses, landlords, the IRS, loan companies, bill collectors — we let these things dictate our worth, but in the long run, they have nothing to do with who we are. The only worthwhile standards for us are *internal,* involving our character, our soul. It's the voice inside we need to listen to, not the voices of the world.

When we listen to and live by our inner voice, we come to know ourselves in a different way and also to know God in a much more loving, intimate way. When we look within, we find every answer we need. When we live by our inner guidance, we are freed from the restrictions of Earth and we come to truly know the magic of life.

It only takes a moment! Go inside, feel the presence of God. It's so calming and peaceful. And it's always there for you. As a child of God, you are entitled to a relationship with that greatness. Know it, talk to it, listen to it, and get all you can from it.

I was about ten years old when I first heard this Bible verse: "Heaven can be entered only through the narrow gate! The road that leads to destruction is broad, and its gate is wide enough for all the multitudes who choose its easy way. But the Gateway to Life is small, and the road is narrow and only a few ever find it" (Matthew 7:13–14). When I first heard that, a distant memory came to mind; I remembered, somehow, that path was the road I came here to walk in this lifetime.

Because the road that leads to God is not an easy one, many people choose the wide road instead — but don't let that happen to you. You're reading this book because you have a sense of the other road, you have a knowingness that says you deserve more than what's going on in your life right now. It may seem easier to follow the crowd and do what everyone else is doing — following what appears to be the safe road in life — but the truth is that road doesn't encourage individuality. Instead, it promotes a deadening conformity, and it keeps you farther away from God.

Throughout the book, we've looked at the various blocks that get in our way of hearing and living by our internal voice. Yesterday in meditation my inner voice said to write about one other block that is perhaps the greatest obstacle for most of us, for it keeps us from hearing the truth and wisdom within us, and that obstacle is our sense of self-worth. Your sense of self-worth, your self-esteem, dictates the good that you allow into your life. If you have a low self-worth, you'll find a way to sabotage all the good that is trying to come to you. If you have a healthy self-worth, you'll allow all of God's blessings to come into your life.

For those of you struggling with self-worth, I have two suggestions: One is to get some good therapy and heal all those issues that keep you from fully, completely, and unconditionally loving yourself; the second is to ask God to help you heal whatever is in your way of living a spiritual way of life.

So many people that come to me ask what the purpose of their life is, and over and over in readings I see that their soul is here to heal their unresolved pain, to gain wisdom from all their life experiences, and to discover unconditional love for themselves and others.

You are not here by accident, my friend. There is a reason your soul has come to earth to experience another lifetime, and it's a great reason. There is nothing small about it. As Nelson Mandela said, no one benefits by you being small. Do whatever it is you need to do to heal. You have a right to be free of any emotional, physical, or mental pain you're in. You deserve every bit of happiness that God intends you to have.

Your birthright as a child of God is to become the best you can be, and you can accomplish that gloriously by listening always to the guidance of the voice within you.

About the Author

Echo Bodine is a renowned psychic, spiritual healer, and teacher. She has appeared on many national TV shows, including *Sally Jesse Raphael*, *Sightings*, *The Other Side* and NBC's *Later Today*. She has written several books: *Echoes of the Soul*, *Hands That Heal*, and *Relax, It's Only a Ghost*.

Echo lectures throughout the country on life, death, life after death, and living by our intuition. She lives in Bloomington, Minnesota.

If you would like information on Echo's other books or meditation tapes you can write to her at:

Echo Bodine
P. O. Box 385321
Bloomington, MN 55438
E-mail: Echo@echobodine.com

If you enjoyed *A Still, Small Voice*, we recommend the following books and cassettes from New World Library.

Creative Visualization by Shakti Gawain. This classic work (in print for twenty years with more than three million copies sold) shows us how to use the power of our imagination to create what we want in life. Also available on audiocassette, in two formats: the complete book on tape, and selected meditations from the book.

Echoes of the Soul by Echo Bodine. Echo first tells the remarkable story of her discovery of her psychic abilities, then tells the truly fascinating and wonderful story of the tour she was given — a great sweeping vision to the worlds "beyond the light." Readers will never look at death or "the afterlife" in the same way.

Living in the Light: A Guide to Personal and Planetary Transformation (revised) by Shakti Gawain, with Laurel King. A newly updated edition of the recognized classic that teaches us how to listen to our intuition and rely on it as a guiding force.

Living in the Light Workbook (revised) by Shakti Gawain and Laurel King. Following up her bestseller, *Living in the Light*, Shakti has created a workbook to help us apply the principles in *Living in the Light* to our lives in very practical ways.

The Individual and the Nature of Mass Events by Jane Roberts. Extending the idea that we create our own reality, Seth explores the connection between personal beliefs and world events.

The Magical Approach by Jane Roberts. Seth discusses how we can live our lives spontaneously, creatively, and according to our own natural rhythms.

Maps to Ecstasy: A Healing Journey for the Untamed Spirit (revised) by Gabrielle Roth, with John Loudon. A modern shaman shows us how to reconnect to the vital energetic core of our being through dance, song, theater, writing, meditation, and ritual.

Miracles of Mind by Russell Targ and Jane Katra, Ph.D. In this inspiring exploration of the mind's power, pioneering physicist Russell Targ and spiritual healer Jane Katra explore how our mind's ability to transcend the limits of time and space is linked to our capacity for healing.

The Nature of Personal Reality by Jane Roberts. Seth explains how the conscious mind directs unconscious activity, and has at its command all the powers of the inner self.

The Path of Transformation: How Healing Ourselves Can Change the World by Shakti Gawain. Bestselling author Shakti Gawain delivers an inspiring and provocative message for the path of true transformation.

Power of Now by Eckhart Tolle. Every moment is miraculous. We realize this when we stop thinking about the past and future, and find the now. This book is powerful. It can change your life instantly in the now moment.

Seth Speaks by Jane Roberts. In this essential guide to conscious living, Seth clearly and powerfully articulates the concept that we create our own reality according to our beliefs.

Still the Mind by Alan Watts. This wonderful book has been transcribed from recordings of several talks he gave in his later years, recorded and edited by his son, Mark Watts. The teachings of Alan Watts show a maturity and wisdom that can only come after years of meditation, and his words are still as visionary today as when they were first spoken. Whether you are experienced in meditation or just beginning, *Still the Mind* takes you on a wonderful journey that shows you the great miracle of who we really are.

Way of the Peaceful Warrior by Dan Millman. This is the story of Dan Millman, a world champion athlete who journeys into realms of romance and magic, light and darkness, body, mind, and spirit. Guided by a wise and powerful old warrior named Socrates, tempted by an elusive, playful woman named Joy, Dan is led toward a final confrontation that will deliver or destroy him.